CAMOUFLAGE
ISN'T ONLY
FOR
COMBAT

Melissa S. Herbert

CAMOUFLAGE ISN'T ONLY FOR COMBAT

GENDER, SEXUALITY, AND WOMEN IN THE MILITARY

NEW YORK UNIVERSITY PRESS

New York and London

NEW YORK UNIVERSITY PRESS
New York and London

Library of Congress Cataloging-in-Publication Data
Herbert, Melissa S., 1956–
Camouflage isn't only for combat : gender, sexuality, and women
in the military / Melissa S. Herbert.
p.   cm.
Includes bibliographical references (p.   ) and index.
ISBN 0-8147-3547-9 (cloth : acid-free paper)
1. United States—Armed Forces—Women. 2. Sociology, Military—
United States. I. Title.
UB418.W65H47   1998
355'.0082—dc21   97-45414
                    CIP

New York University Press books are printed on acid-free paper,
and their binding materials are chosen for strength and durability.

Manufactured in the United States of America

10   9   8   7   6   5   4   3   2   1

CONTENTS

ACKNOWLEDGMENTS

One of the few certainties in life is that a project such as this cannot be completed without the assistance of others. Members of the Department of Sociology at the University of Arizona provided me with invaluable support for this project. Each member of my dissertation committee, Paula England, Pat MacCorquodale, Doug McAdam, and Jim Shockey, provided unique contributions to the conduct and completion of this research. I must also thank members of the Department of Sociology at the University of Massachusetts at Amherst, where I began my graduate training, especially Peter Rossi, who showed me that survey research was alive and well, and Gene Fisher and Jay Demerath, for telling me to "go for it" when others wished to convince me otherwise. Special thanks go to Ruth A. Wallace of The George Washington University. Without her support and encouragement I would never have rediscovered sociology. I would be remiss were I not to thank my departmental colleagues at Hamline University, Martin Markowitz, Maggie Jensen, and Navid Mohseni, for their continued support and good humor.

This research received partial support from a University of Arizona Graduate College Summer Research Support grant, as well as a University of Arizona Department of Sociology Dissertation Award. I also wish to acknowledge the support of the Women's Studies Advisory Council, whose grants enabled me to present my work at various professional meetings. I am also grateful for the Hanna Grant I received from Hamline University, which enabled me to conduct in-depth interviews, and for additional funding for computing resources from the Dean of the College of Liberal Arts.

I must thank my family, especially my parents, Ralph and Priscilla Walker, for always believing in me. Many friends and colleagues have freely given their support as well, especially Douglas Adams, Jennifer Eichstedt, and Daniel Jones. Thanks must also go to Katie Krile and Mackenzie Hickman, students at Hamline University who assisted in the preparation of final drafts of the manuscript.

I must acknowledge the assistance of the many wonderful people I have "met" on the listserv of The MINERVA Center, especially those who responded to my requests for verification of facts or figures. Special mention goes to Linda Grant De-Pauw of The George Washington University for establishing and maintaining The MINERVA Center. For those of us interested in women and the military, it is an incredibly valuable resource.

Thanks as well to Jennifer Hammer at New York University Press, whose editing was nothing short of miraculous. Never did I expect to actually agree with almost every change an editor might suggest! I am grateful as well to Niko Pfund, who expressed interest in the project long before it even resembled a dissertation.

Needless to say, without the participation of hundreds of women this project would not have been possible, and I thank them as well. I hope that, while some will see themselves in this story more clearly than others, they will each feel that at least a part of their voice is reflected.

1

INTRODUCTION

> I was ashamed to admit that I'd been in the service because I *knew* what the assumptions about my character would be. There was certainly no pride felt in my family about my service. There was grief when I went in, and I think some embarrassment. "Nice" girls didn't join the Army.
>
> —Major, Army, heterosexual

Since the 1940s, when women began to enter the military in significant numbers, questions have been raised about their intent, their ability, and, perhaps most frequently, their character. It was believed that a woman who would place herself in an environment that was both numerically and ideologically "male" must either be looking for a husband or for multiple sexual partners or must wish that she were, in fact, male. But, while the focus on the military may have been new, questions about women's participation in domains previously defined as male were not. When women first sought to attend college, it was widely believed that education might damage a woman's reproductive system. When women sought to participate in sport, similar fears were expressed. In addition, as with the military, concern was voiced about what kind of women might want to participate in such activities in the first place.

When women seek to enter male domains, they are often confronted by societal expectations concerning what constitutes a "real woman." Surely a "real woman" doesn't want to carry a weapon, sleep in a foxhole, or go for weeks without a shower. A "real woman" doesn't want to do "men things." Sociocultural notions of what constitutes femininity and masculinity are used to insure that women who push the boundaries of gender are censured for such behaviors. While one mechanism is the threat that they are somehow less than "real women," another is the threat of labeling them "lesbian." A "real woman" does not do that most manly of "men things," sleep with women. Gender and sexuality are intertwined in such a way that notions of appropriateness in one are used to reinforce the other.

Many women who have entered the military have done so with the disapproval of friends and family. While this is certainly not the case for all women, and is less the case today, the perception that women who would enter the military were not "nice girls" was at one time quite widespread.

In 1942, shortly before the establishment of the Women's Army Auxiliary Corps, civilian and military personnel alike expressed concern over the type of women who might join such an organization. Many believed that women who would be interested in the military would be either fierce, masculine women wishing to act like men or delicate, feminine women who, presumably, were unfit for such service. In response, Mrs. Oveta Culp Hobby, chief of the women's interests section of the War Department's Bureau of Public Relations, said that the members of the proposed corps would be neither "Amazons rushing into battle" nor "butterflies fluttering free" ("Freedom of Press" 1942). Yet, it seemed impossible for the corps's critics to imagine that reality might lay somewhere between these two extremes.[1]

The confusion over what women doing "men's" work meant prompted a full-scale campaign to assure women, their families, and men, as well, that, "though the economy required that women assume male roles, don functional clothing, and engage in physically demanding dirty work . . . these new roles did not signify fundamental changes in the sexual orientation of women themselves or in their customary image as sex objects" (Honey 1984: 114). A memo from the Office of Emergency Management addressed these fears, as well:

> There is an unwholesomely large number of girls who refrain from even contemplating enlistment because of male opinion. An educative program needs to be done among the male population to overcome this problem. Men—both civilian and military personnel—should be specifically informed that it is fitting for girls to be in the service. This would call for copy . . . which shows that the services increase, rather than detract from, desirable feminine characteristics. (Honey 1984: 113)

Interestingly, the military—or at least the folks who handle advertising for the Army—are aware that such conflicts about female and male roles continue and may affect recruiting. A recent recruiting advertisement shows a woman in front of a helicopter, wearing her flight helmet, lipstick, and mascara. The emphasized text, larger and boxed, is a phrase that the Army has been using for a while now: "There's something about a soldier." The text surrounding this statement reads:

> Especially if you're a woman. Because you'll find yourself doing the most amazing things. Like being a flight Crew Chief or a Topographic Surveyor, or any one of nearly 200 skills the Army offers. You'll also find yourself doing some very familiar things. Like getting into aerobics, going to the movies or just being with friends. The point is, *a woman in the Army is still a woman* [italics mine].(*Rolling Stone* 26 January 1995)

A smaller photo at the bottom of the page shows the same woman wearing civilian clothes, large hoop earrings, and a large ring and with a young man with his arm around her. Clearly, this advertisement is trying to reassure women that they can do "male" things like being a flight crew chief or a topographic surveyor and still "be a woman."

During the last decade, and particularly in the wake of armed conflict involving female military personnel, interest in the role of women in the military has increased dramatically. Issues concerning women in the military have been the subject of both academic and governmental inquiry, as well as the object of media attention. These issues range from whether women veterans experience a pay premium as a result of military service to the role of women in combat. Scholarly works have been written around these issues, some providing a general overview of the experience of women in the military, others focusing on specific experiences such as attendance at

West Point, being a lesbian in the military, or serving in Vietnam, to provide a glimpse into the lives of those women.

While these works do capture what life is like for many women in the military, few have examined how women in the military negotiate an environment that has been both structured and defined as "masculine." The emphasis has been on *what* the women experience, rather than *how they manage* that experience. This book focuses on this latter question, examining how gender and sexuality interact to shape how women manage life in the military.

Women currently constitute about 13 percent of the United States military. There is little question that women have made inroads into the military hierarchy that would have been difficult to imagine even a decade ago. In 1993, Sheila Widnall became the first woman appointed to head one of the branches of the military. Although the position of secretary of the Air Force is a civilian post, this appointment may reflect a new wave of acceptance of women in military leadership. It was also during 1993 that women first attended combat pilot training, and in 1994 women received their first permanent assignments to Navy warships. And, in June 1997, Claudia J. Kennedy became the first woman in the Army to be promoted to the rank of lieutenant general. Nonetheless, for reasons that are both institutional and interpersonal, women remain marginalized within all military settings.

Debate over women's marginalization in the military has often centered on institutional factors such as restrictions on women in nontraditional occupations within the military, including combat exclusion policies. Examination of the possibility that interpersonal barriers exist have, for the most part, focused on issues such as sexual harassment and individual discrimination.

The existence of institutional constraints can be confirmed by examining military regulations, while interpersonal constraints can be observed in women's continued experiences of sexual harassment and discrimination at the individual level. Recent cases of harassment involving personnel ranging from recruits at training facilities to the sergeant major of the army are evidence enough that the problem remains. Both institutional and interpersonal barriers derive at least in part from a gender ideology that views military service as the domain of men and that affirms masculinity as one mechanism by which men become soldiers. I believe that it is this broader ideology that is much more effective in limiting the participation of women in the military than either specific institutional or interpersonal constraints.

A lengthy history associates men with the public sphere of paid work, or production, and women with the private sphere of nonpaid work, or reproduction. Whether by consigning them to "female" jobs or fighting their access to "male" jobs, women have been confronted with challenges to their "right" to participate in the labor force on an equal basis with men. Rather than look to neoclassical arguments about how women make different choices from men or about the illogic of discrimination, I posit that much of this confrontation is situated in a conflict over gender ideology and the "appropriateness" of certain jobs for women. Nowhere does this issue seem to generate as much debate as in the military.

We have seen attempts to change the regulations or improve the enforcement of existing policies on harassment and discrimination. I believe, however, that women in the military face a much more difficult task than changing regulations or policies. Even with changes that now make it possible for women to fly fighter aircraft or serve on warships, women continue to face harassment and discrimination at the individual level. Much as in the case of eliminating racism, there is what we might call the "de facto" response (e.g., ignoring the formal penalties), as well as the "de jure" response (e.g., formalizing penalties for sexual harassment).

In her essay on "gendered institutions," Joan Acker writes that this term "means that gender is present in the processes, practice, images and ideologies, and distributions of power in the various sectors of social life" (1992: 567). The military is a "gendered institution" because soldiering has been about not only war, but being "a man." On a more practical level, the military is gendered in that rules about who can hold what jobs and serve in what areas are structured along the lines of gender, not age, race, or physical fitness. Elsewhere, Acker writes that "organizations are one arena in which widely disseminated cultural images of gender are invented and reproduced" (1990: 140). This, I argue, is the case with the military and constructions of gender.

Organizations are gendered in that they both reflect and contribute to the gendered nature of the broader social structure. Women and men in the military, not unlike those in other organizations, are certain to experience organizational life differently. Although the military is in many ways unique, it is certainly not immune to the processes I have described.

In fact, there appears to be little dispute over the tradition of soldiering as a male bastion. The complex weaving together of the achievement of manhood or masculinity with military service offers us insight into the way in which the notion of soldiering has historically been so central a part of male identity. It makes sense that the reverse would be true, that maleness is so central a part of soldiering.

Prior to the elimination of the draft, the military represented a part of traditional sex-role identity for American men, as well as a primary socialization agent for this identity. Even with the advent of the all-volunteer force and the integration of women into the military, this connection was not entirely broken. A video used by the Selective Service System to brief new members contains a theme song whose refrain is, "I want to call you mister, but I can't until you register." This lyric highlights the relationship between manhood and military service. It should, however, be acknowledged that such beliefs developed throughout history when, with few exceptions, soldiers were all men, and most men became soldiers.

Proclamation of sexual prowess is also evident in the military, specifically in settings that are predominantly male. Not only does the "locker room" talk of high school continue, but cadences that brag about the sexual conquering of women can still be heard in all male settings. And, songs, riddles, and rituals that denigrate women continue (Burke 1996). It is not enough to simply be male; one must be "more male" than the men in the next squad, platoon, and so forth.

Neither is it enough to rely on sexual prowess and physical ability to establish one's masculinity and, thus, one's status as a soldier. Much of the strategy seems to rely on being that which is not feminine and, taking this one step further, denigrating that which is feminine. Erving Goffman notes, "A considerable amount of what persons who are men do in affirmation of their sense of identity requires their doing something that can be seen as what a woman by her nature could not do, or at least could not do well" (1977: 326). Even in the absence of the draft and with the increased participation of women in the military, it seems clear that, for many, the military continues to be viewed as one option for the expression of masculinity and the achievement of manhood.

Although the stated goal of basic training is to transform civilians into soldiers, another objective, as I have suggested, has been to transform boys into men. The literature, fictitious (e.g., *The Red Badge of Courage*) as well as scholarly, is rife with examples of military service as a means by which one's masculinity is confirmed.

The process of basic training is one of depersonalization and deindividuation in which the military, in the form of drill sergeants, must strip the individual of all previous self-definition. While basic training is intended to teach one the skills needed to perform as a soldier, it is also intended to vest each participant with a clear notion of what it means to *be* a soldier, a Marine, and so forth.[2] In the case of military training, these images are characteristically male. As almost all young men throughout the first three-quarters of the twentieth century had to complete some form of military service, basic training can be seen as having been the male equivalent of "finishing school."

One of the most common ways to bolster masculinity by denigrating femininity is the use of slang descriptors of females or female anatomy (e.g., "skirt," "pussy") and non-slang descriptors (e.g., women, girls) to characterize and belittle males. The best challenge to one's masculinity is the "accusation" of femininity.

Clearly, masculinity in military men not only is rewarded but is the primary construct around which resocialization as a soldier takes place. It is not, then, surprising that femininity, or characteristics believed to be associated with femininity, would be discouraged. On the other hand, the military, reflecting the broader society, may find that maintaining women's femininity serves to reinforce notions of what it means to be "a man." That is, by requiring women to maintain a degree of femininity, perceptions of masculinity remain intact. This may be well illustrated by the old Navy and Marine Corps policies in which female recruits received makeup and etiquette training.

The military is a highly traditional, primarily conservative institution in which we may expect the expression, "men are men and women are women" to be taken seriously. Exactly how are women in the military supposed to "be women"? The integration of women into an institution *defined* by its association with masculinity has posed an interesting dilemma for military women. Can one truly be a soldier and a woman and not be viewed as deviating either from what it means to be a soldier or from what it means to be a woman?

In their article "Doing Gender," Candace West and Don Zimmerman "propose an ethnomethodologically informed ... understanding of gender[3] as a routine, methodical, and recurring accomplishment" (1987: 126). Rather than a state of being—e.g., you *are* feminine, you *are* masculine—gender is performed. We enact femininity and masculinity; we don't simply *become* feminine or masculine. They also maintain that "gender itself is constituted through interaction" (1987: 129). It is the actions that are socially defined as feminine or masculine, others' responses to those actions and the actor's response to those responses—interaction—that assigns meaning to our behaviors. This framing of the concept of "doing gender" as both ethnomethodologically informed and interactional in nature draws upon two theoretical traditions: "ethnomethodology" and "symbolic interactionism."

Ethnomethodology has its roots in phenomenology, the idea that we can never know more about something than what we can experience through our senses. Ethnomethodology[4] can be defined as social actors' methods for making sense of the world around them. Key to this approach is "to treat as problematic what is taken for granted in order to understand the commonsense everyday world" (Wallace and Wolf 1991: 295). This method is particularly appropriate for any inquiry into gender. Because of its perceived relation to biology (i.e., whether one is identified as female or male), gender, as traditionally conceived, is often seen as fixed. That is, females are feminine, males are masculine. By constructing gender as problematic, by questioning the social "facts" of gender, we employ an ethnomethodological perspective.

Although it has been said that Erving Goffman did not consider himself a symbolic interactionist, his work is very much a part of that perspective. In his study of mental institutions, Goffman found that "inmates invented many ingenious strategies to preserve their own selfhood rather than surrender to an acceptance of the role and the self that the institution prescribes" (Wallace and Wolf 1991: 274). The ability of the actor to not only adjust to the demands of the situation but to preserve the self is of particular interest when we look at women in the military. Not only is the military a total institution whose members undergo a process of deindividuation, but, for women, there is the question of whether they are somehow "de-gendered." Women may not only "do gender" to reconcile conflicting roles but may do so to help maintain a sense of self in an otherwise alienating, and sometimes hostile, setting.

Gender, then, is something we "do" rather than something we simply "are." If we wish to examine gender as interactional, as an active process rather than a passive acquisition, then it is helpful to understand the contributions of symbolic interactionism to the development of such a perspective. West and Zimmerman's conception of gender is not strictly symbolic interactionist, yet it draws heavily on notions of interaction and the work of Goffman. As such, this perspective is critical to any approach in which gender is viewed as an interactional accomplishment.

Actions are undertaken, among other reasons, "with an eye to how they might be assessed (e.g., as 'womanly' or 'manly' behaviors)" (West and Fenstermaker 1995: 21). Accountability is important to our ability to make sense not only to ourselves, but to those around us. Women are likely involved in creating gender not simply "for gender's sake" but to show that they are women, that they are adhering to normative conceptions of femaleness. When the issue is gender, it is not simply whether we are, for example, female and our actions viewed as appropriate for females, but whether the action is viewed as appropriate to the setting in which we are observed.

For women, this may provide the ultimate contradiction. Given the masculine nature of the military, female soldiers may be accountable not only as women but as soldiers/pseudomen. How do women make sense of this apparent contradiction? How do women maintain a sense of order in a world in which the expectations placed upon them may be seen by many as contradicting one another?

Where ethnomethodology addresses the broad question of making sense of the world around us, "doing gender" addresses the more focused question of how we make sense of our status as females or males. But, as evidenced by the question just posed, such an inquiry cannot be undertaken without an eye to the situation in which such interaction takes place.

"While individuals are the ones who do gender, the process of rendering something accountable is both interactional and institutional in character: it is a feature of social relationships, and its idiom derives from the institutional arena in which those relationships come to life" (West and Fenstermaker 1995: 21). While the claim that we *do* gender is not limited to a particular situational context, the *way* in which we do gender is very much shaped by the situation. A woman in a male-dominated setting may do gender in a very different way from a woman in a setting that is not structured by ideas rooted in masculine ideology.

This book examines how women in the male-dominated world of the military manage gender and sexuality. I begin with the assumption that women are held accountable as women and as soldiers. Given that soldiering has been, and continues to be, constructed as a male pursuit, this dual accountability presents women with a conundrum of sorts. What kind of actions, or strategies, do women employ to be accepted as women soldiers?

The concept of "doing gender" is useful because the actions or strategies that female soldiers employ are selected largely on the basis of the perceptions that result. They know they will be held accountable, both as women and as soldiers. What effect will a given action have on the way in which they are perceived? These choices are interactional in that they are shaped, not simply by socialization or the internalization of gender norms, but with a conscious eye to their consequences. Thus, their everyday actions (e.g., choice of uniform, hobby, or social activity) involve the creation and re-creation of what it means to be a woman, particularly a woman soldier. They are doing gender.

In addition to the question of individual action, there is the question of the role of gender in the creation or maintenance of the institution. As I have indicated, gender is a great deal more than a role or a static characteristic. The way in which we create and recreate what it means to be feminine or masculine, or something in between, leads to gender's being not simply a descriptor but a structure in and of itself.

At one time the military was entirely male. Women accompanied the military as seamstresses, cooks, and so on, but they were not recognized as military personnel. Even when women first "entered" the military, it was as auxiliary members. Only in the 1970s did women begin to function as integrated members of the heretofore male military organization. Thus, it is not surprising that the "work-role" of the military was defined in terms of men and masculinity. Furthermore, the use of masculinity to socialize new recruits into the role of soldier reinforces the bond between "maleness" and "soldiering," further solidifying the bond between masculinity and the role of soldier.

The military, as an institution, is faced with a conflict. Which is more important, accomplishment of the mission by those most capable or maintenance of a gender ideology in which military service and the role of the warrior must remain predominantly, if not exclusively, male? To address this question, we must first turn our attention to the role of sexuality within the military.

Many studies have examined the experiences of women in male-dominated occupations and industries, generally exploring issues such as promotion, wages, tokenism, and sexual harassment. While such inquiries may require that one examine issues of sex and sexuality, they do not necessarily mandate an examination of the *integration* of sexuality into the construction of the occupation or industry itself. In the broader society, sexuality, and the values and norms that we apply to it, are used to confine people to prescribed gender roles. Such a mechanism also exists within occupations and institutions.

Sexuality can be used to construct a model of prescribed behavior in some occupations in which employees are "kept in line" by defining acceptable boundaries of sexuality and gender norms. There are two ways in which the military attempts to control sexuality among its members. One is through the real, as well as imagined, segregation of women and men in the military environment.

In the late 1970s and early 1980s, the U.S. Army experimented with sex-integrated basic training. Women and men received basic training together. Sleeping quarters were separate, but down to the squad level, women and men trained together. In 1983 the U.S. Army returned to sex-segregated basic training. According to a senior military official at the U.S. Army Training and Doctrine Command who was involved in the decision-making process on this issue, the primary reason for ending sex-integrated training was the perceived problem of fraternization between female and male soldiers. However, the "public" story focused on the belief that the presence of women lowered the standards, thereby making the men's training easier, in reality a secondary concern at best.

In some instances, the belief that strict segregation is maintained is nothing more than myth. It is not uncommon for women and men to share tents while billeted in the field. In some settings (e.g., security sites) women and men sleep in the same room to maintain squad integrity. The most common form of shared facilities is probably the latrine. In buildings where there is only one latrine for a large area, the practice has evolved of either having a "one-sex" latrine that is regulated by signs on the door (i.e., male occupied, female occupied, not occupied) or using the latrine together except during shower times. It may well be that the custom of separate facilities is not so much demanded by the existence of two sexes as it is a means of reinforcing perceptions of sex/gender differences. Control of sexuality may, in fact, not be so much a result of gender differences as it is a mechanism for insuring their maintenance.

As anyone who has served in the military will attest, "where there's a will, there's a way." It is not uncommon for relationships to form quickly and with great intensity, especially during the stress of basic training, when communication with friends and family is severely restricted. Interestingly, this is seen as desirable when the two soldiers are heterosexual, same-sex "buddies." Camaraderie and unit cohesion are seen as primary goals of the training process. Readers may recall the repeated emphasis on the importance of unit cohesion during the Senate hearings on lesbians and gays in the military. Yet, when such a relationship is romantic rather than platonic, whether between women and men or between homosexual pairs, it is seen as threatening. One way to eliminate this threat is to remove the opportunity for women and men to engage in such relationships. The military believes that it accomplishes this with heterosexuals by segregating women and men and by having strict rules about adultery and fraternization.

Another mechanism for controlling sexuality is the prohibition of lesbians and gay men from military service. The argument that the military does not allow men and women to share a barracks room or latrine was raised in the recent debate over lesbians and gays in the military. The quick follow to this claim was that the military could, then, hardly be expected to allow a woman who was attracted to women to live with a woman, or a man who was attracted to men with a man. By believing that they have successfully controlled heterosexuality *and* by deploying the myth that women and men really are segregated in sleeping and bath accommodations, military leaders were able to suggest that to allow lesbians and gays in the military would give them privileges not available to heterosexuals.

Needless to say, the ban on lesbians and gay men does not keep all homosexuals out of the military. But, it may, in fact, serve to reinforce notions both of masculinity and femininity and of what is acceptable for members of either sex. Such policies may, in fact, be based not so much on alleged damage to "good order and morale" but rather on the challenge to traditional gender roles.

In a memo dated July 24, 1990, Vice Admiral Joseph S. Donnell of the U.S. Navy directed the officers of approximately two hundred ships and forty shore installations to vigorously enforce the policy of discharging any woman found to be a lesbian. He went on to say that he suspected that such investigations may be "pursued halfheartedly" by commanders because lesbian sailors are generally "hard-working, career-oriented, willing to put in long hours on the job, and among the command's top performers" (Gross 1990: 24). Given this view at the top, it is not difficult to imagine the erroneous characterization of some heterosexual sailors as lesbians because they are hardworking, career oriented, and willing to put in long hours on the job. The policy of exclusion does not only affect lesbians. As a female drill instructor stated during a Parris Island witch hunt for lesbian Marines, "The qualities and traits that we demand and are supposed to be training our recruits are the same traits that make us look homosexual" (Shilts 1993: 596).

Homophobia is a weapon of sexism that affects all women.[5] The primary means by which this fear is manifest is the attribution of sexuality based on perceived violations of sex-appropriate behaviors. Whether in athletics, the women's movement, nontraditional civilian occupations, or the military, regardless of one's view of one's own sexual orientation, the threat or the label of "lesbian" is used as a mechanism, or a weapon, of control. Sometimes the boundaries intersect. One woman wrote that she "quit playing on post-sponsored athletic teams" to avoid being suspected of being lesbian or bisexual. Another was warned by her first sergeant that if she played softball, she would be viewed as a lesbian. Women who display behaviors, attitudes, or simply a demeanor viewed as "male" are often immediately suspect. One woman wrote, "I believe any woman who is perceived as 'masculine' or 'too masculine' is thought to be a lesbian—regardless of marital status/children." One need not be a lesbian to experience discrimination based on homophobia.

Given that our society does not encourage, and in most instances discourages, the open acknowledgement of lesbianism, why do some women get labeled as lesbian, while others do not? I, like others, argue that it is violations of broader social understandings about gender that serve as markers for one's perceived sexual orientation. In a society in which many behaviors are clearly perceived as feminine or masculine, those who cross such boundaries are subject to censure in the form of having their sexual orientation questioned. As Maria Lowe (1993) points out in her study of female bodybuilding, in nontraditional endeavors conceptions of femininity are often used to restrict women's participation. In the film *Pumping Iron II: The Women*, we see officials wrestling over how to balance notions of appropriate femininity in a sport where "the best" was previously defined more simply as the man with the largest, most well-defined musculature. In the competition shown in the film, the woman who is clearly the largest, and perhaps most well defined, is penalized by the judges for violating the boundaries of femininity. It is circumstances such as these that are critical to our understanding of the position of women in an occupational setting in which being successful may require that one possess a number of "masculine" characteristics.

In their experimental work on homosexuality, Mary E. Kite and Kay Deaux (1987) found that some of the most frequently mentioned attributes for the condition "female homosexual" were those labels deemed by many to be characteristic of military women: masculine mannerisms or appearance, short hair, wearing of masculine clothing, and athleticism. They concluded that homosexual stereotypes are largely defined by gender. Randy Shilts writes, "Although clerk/typists were as likely to be lesbian, they were rarely suspect; mechanics almost always were. Husky women were suspicious; petite women were not" (1993: 496).

The attribution of homosexuality to those who violate gender norms is not new. Historical evidence suggests that women who performed men's tasks, wore men's clothing, or refused to attach themselves to men have long been subject to the label of "lesbian." Julia Perez, an Army veteran, tells us what her attorney was told when she asked a witness what made her think Perez was a homosexual. The witness said, "She's got her hair cut short, I've seen her wear flats with her uniform, she's very masculine . . ." (1987: 56). What happens when the same attributes (e.g., masculinity) that are seen as desirable for success in the occupation or industry (e.g., military/soldiering) are also those that lead a group (e.g., women) to be labeled with a characteristic (e.g., lesbian) deemed unacceptable for participation in the occupation?

The military is an "institutionalized arena" in which the masculine is preferred over the feminine, and men are preferred over women. A female military police officer in the U.S. Army stated, "It's still a male-oriented military, and no matter how hard you work, or how good your reputation is, you're a woman, and you get slighted for being one" (Barkalow 1990: 251). It is one thing for women to enter occupations which have previously been defined as "male"; it is another to enter an occupation in which masculinity is so central a part of the definition of the occupation. Men have traditionally been the firefighters, the construction workers, and the corporate executive officers, and requirements for "male" attributes such as courage, physical strength, or assertiveness have often been used to exclude women. This happens in many occupations, yet in few of these occupations is masculinity itself, and all aspects of its construction, seen as so fundamental to the ability to perform the job. In the case of the military, it is clear that women must fill a work role that is male defined. How do these women reconcile the male-defined work role with the expectation that their "gender" is "feminine"? The underlying thesis of the work presented here is that women in the military are faced with the problem of having to strike a balance between femininity and masculinity.

Women who enter a male-dominant setting must learn how to redefine and manage "femaleness." One strategy for this process, blending, "depends on a very careful management of being 'feminine enough' . . . while simultaneously being 'businesslike enough'" (Sheppard 1989: 146). To be perceived as "too feminine" may mean being perceived as incompetent or weak, while being perceived as "too masculine" may mean being perceived as a lesbian. An etiquette manual from 1960 points out a different contradiction. "A woman in business is supposed to be a woman, not one of the boys. On the other hand, you must avoid being so female that you embarrass your co-workers" (Bevans 1960: 69). In her work on lesbians in the corporate world, Marny Hall states, "We can expect women who define themselves as lesbian in this culture to have developed strategies to maneuver in inimical environments" (1986: 71). At their extreme, women sometimes fabricate boyfriends or adopt "covers"—men who pretend to be more than friends. While the strategies employed by lesbians and bisexual women may differ from those employed by heterosexual women, all women in male-dominated occupations must develop strategies to negotiate the hostile terrain of the workplace. What exactly is it that women must do to function in the military and not risk censure?

A woman may attempt to minimize her femininity and be "one of the guys." Women "do not want to draw attention to themselves as women. . . . Thus, they defeminize their gender roles, emphasize their work status, and distance themselves from other women" (Dunivin 1988: 60). This is much like the blending strategy described earlier.

On the other hand, a woman may "play up" her femininity and thus attempt to convey the message that she is not a threat to men's jobs or status. In some instances, this strategy may include distancing herself from other women whom she feels aren't "feminine enough." Lowe finds that "female bodybuilders . . . consciously construct their femininity to such an extent that they distance themselves from 'deviant' female bodybuilders who are too 'unfeminine' and too muscular" (1993: 12). Some research even finds that individuals may have "two different gender identity images—one they consider descriptive of their at-home situation and another of their at-work situation" (Chusmir and Koberg 1990: 546).

At its core, this book seeks to address four questions. First, do women believe that the military pressures or encourages women to be "more masculine" or "more feminine" than might otherwise be the case? That is, do women in the military believe that they are placed in the situation of having to be "masculine enough" to be seen as capable of doing the job but "feminine enough" not to have their gender identity and/or sexual orientation questioned? Second, are there penalties for being perceived as being "too masculine" or "too feminine"? If so, what might these penalties be? Third, do women's experiences and/or attitudes differ with their sexual orientation? Finally, how is it, if at all, that women employ strategies that allow them to function in the male-dominated world of the military? In what ways do they "do" gender and sexuality?

To answer these questions I conducted quantitative and qualitative analyses of 285 surveys completed by women who have served in the U.S. military or were still serving at the time they completed the survey. The women served as early as 1957 and spent from one to thirty-two years on active duty. Women entered active duty as young as seventeen and as late as forty. Respondents' current ages ranged from twenty to sixty-five. Women from all four branches were represented. The sample contained 184 women whose highest rank was as an enlisted person and 101 women whose highest rank was as an officer. Two hundred and twelve women currently identify as heterosexual and seventy-three as lesbian or bisexual. In addition to the surveys, I conducted in-depth interviews with fourteen women, all except one of whom had previously completed the survey. Additional details on methodology are contained in the Appendix.

Chapter 2 addresses the question of femininity and masculinity and the question of how women believe gender perceptions affect their participation in the military. Here I address whether or not women believe that penalties exist for those who violate gender norms and, if so, what these penalties might be.

In chapter 3 I turn to a discussion of sexuality. How does sexuality interact with gender to shape women's experiences? For example, are threats about sexuality (e.g., sexual orientation, sexual availability) used to enforce the "rules" about gender? If so, how? How, if at all, might one's own sexual orientation affect the choices one makes about gender management?

Chapter 4 examines the strategies or "patterns of accommodation" employed by women in the military. In this chapter I focus on the primary question of this research—how women "do gender" and manage sexuality within the context of the military.

In chapter 5 I address the implications of this research, in particular, how these findings allow us to understand the theoretical formulation that has been called "doing gender."

This research contributes not only to our knowledge of the situation of women in the military but, more broadly, to our understanding of the lives of women in male occupations and, even more broadly, to our understanding of the ways in which women "do gender" in all social settings. Specifically, how do women negotiate the dilemmas that come about when to do one's job may mean being perceived as violating gender norms? How are such conflicts resolved when such perceptions may lead to the loss of one's job? What are the results if women "do gender" within the boundaries of normative conceptions of "femininity?" Can they simultaneously assume a "masculine" work role? Answers to these questions will improve our understanding not only of the role of women in the military but of their role in other settings as well.

In addition, and perhaps most important, this research increases our understanding of the importance of the intersections between gender and sexuality that occur throughout our lives. "Sexuality is a common link that reveals the precariousness of gender management" (Sheppard 1989: 156). Kite and Deaux claim that "sexuality has been a generally ignored aspect of gender stereotypes" and argue for "a further broadening of the gender belief net to include sexuality as an important component" (1987: 94). I hope to add not only to our knowledge of how women negotiate institutional and interpersonal barriers on the job but to our knowledge of how these barriers have as their foundation a complex interweaving of social constructions of gender and sexuality.

AMAZONS AND BUTTERFLIES

Gender and the Military

> If you're too feminine, then you're not
> strong enough to command respect and lead
> men into battle, but if you're strong and ag-
> gressive you're not being a woman. It's like a
> double standard.
>
> —Captain, Air Force, lesbian

The Acquisition of Gender

There is little disagreement that the recognition of sex, and subsequently gender, is critical to the organization of daily life. Even the youngest of children are well aware of what constitute "girl things" and "boy things" and that knowing what and who fits where is critical. Small children are quick to question those who do not fit the rules. "Are you a boy?" a three-year-old asked a woman. When asked why he thought the woman was a boy, he responded, "Because she always wears pants." A great many of the "rules" have changed.

Women wear pants, men have long hair, police "men" are women, nurses are men, and so on. Nonetheless, we still struggle to assign gender norms to many of the activities that govern our daily lives.

For many years, and by many people even today, gendered behaviors were considered to be "natural" extensions of one's sex, one's status as females or males. Functionalism "explained" that it made sense that women would provide the bulk of child care and men would be the breadwinners. Women, after all, did bear the children. Men, of course, were stronger and better suited to tackling the demands of labor. Although these arguments no longer dominate the discourse on gender, they are adhered to by some with great tenacity and continue to influence public debate over the roles of women and men in our society.

Whether the argument is over reproductive rights or sexual harassment, notions of what is "natural" for women and men continue to shape our experiences, both publicly and privately. The continuing debate over the origin of gendered behaviors (i.e., nature vs. nurture) is evidence of this fact. Both academic research and popular culture continue to explore questions such as: Are boys "naturally" more aggressive than girls? Are girls "naturally" more nurturing than boys? Do differences in academic skills have their foundation in our biology? And so on. Even with a definitive answer seemingly impossible, the quest goes on.

Regardless of what research reveals, it seems clear that the answers we believe to be correct shape much of our perspective on the roles of women and men in society. This is especially so when the question is whether or not women can or should fill the role of warrior. If women are the "caregivers" of society, should they be in a role that may require them to kill or be killed? If women are more nurturing, can they be expected to fill the military role successfully? Our beliefs about the naturalness of gender influence how we answer these questions.

Throughout the twentieth century, women have struggled to eliminate barriers that blocked them from full participation in a number of settings. While this book focuses on the occupational setting of the military, it is virtually impossible to distinguish between the rules that govern who we are as women and men on any given job and those that define who we are when we are not on the job. The general rules about gender carry over to the workplace and structure what we experience there.

The way in which specific occupations become gendered has been described as "sex-role spillover" (Gutek, Larwood, and Stromberg 1986). "Sex-role spillover" suggests that people endow a job with the sex-role expectations of the numerically dominant sex. When an occupation comes to be seen as "female" or "male," it is then easy to assume that one's ability to do that work is somehow "natural." A by-product of this perspective may be the assumption that those who are not "naturally" suited are not, in fact, capable of doing the job at all.

Male-dominated occupations not only affirm masculinity but become vested with cultural and psychological significance. "Jobs have mystiques, auras . . . attached to them that go well beyond the content of their tasks. Jobs bring their occupants prestige or dishonor, a sense of being manly or womanly . . ." (Epstein 1990: 91) Not only may occupations become gendered because of who fills them, but the occupation itself may come to have a gendered meaning, whether cultural or psychological. All of these processes combine with ideas about the naturalness of gender to establish firm ideas about the degree to which women and men are suited for specific tasks.

Many believe that the role of warrior, protector, and defender of the nation should be reserved for men and men alone. The many arguments for the exclusion of women, which are not addressed in detail here, are situated within two broad positions. The first holds that women are simply not capable of fulfilling the role of warrior. This position encompasses everything from perceived physical limitations to the emotional sphere. The second position maintains that "war" is man's natural role. As women are to bear children, men are obliged to protect the women and children. Many believe that to deny men this role is to somehow disrupt the "natural order of things."

Though there is a lack of consensus over what is "right," we must consider the notion of gender as natural if we are to understand the power of perceived gender roles. An underlying premise of this work is that there is a certain, albeit varying, degree of resistance to the participation of women in the military. In order to understand that resistance, we must give some thought to its roots. This is not to say that we can fully understand or explain gender inequality. To claim as much would be foolish. Rather, we need at least to consider what factors lead some to believe that women should not have access to certain occupational arenas. Much of this contestation is situated in beliefs over what is appropriate for women and men and to what degree these beliefs are rooted in ideas about what is natural.

Consider the following excerpt from a letter to the Opinion Page of the *Navy Times*. "So the U.S. Navy is having a problem with sexual harassment. Well, what does anyone expect? *When women go where they do not belong*, sexual harassment is the logical result" ("Sexual Harassment" 1992: 22, italics mine). While I cannot speculate on the origins of this reader's attitudes, it is clear that he has some firm ideas about what should be expected when women seek and obtain access to areas "where they do not belong."

Beliefs rooted in notions of naturalness are difficult to overcome. There are two related reasons for this resistance. One, even in the face of anecdotal evidence to the contrary, we cannot provide conclusive research that falsifies the argument. Two, even in the presence of "science," ideas of naturalness are resistant to change because such change would seriously call into question beliefs that, for many, have ordered their very existence.

Another perspective on gender is that it is not natural but is socially constructed. Rather than seeing gender as a natural part of who we are as females or males, the social constructionist perspective argues that we create gender, or what it means to be women or men. That is, notions of "femininity" and "masculinity" are created socially and culturally. While this, I argue, is more convincing than the "gender as natural" perspective, it, too, is problematic because many have come to see the acquisition of gender (i.e., possessing feminine or masculine traits) as highly, and often necessarily, correlated with being female or male.

This social constructionist perspective can be used both to deny and support the participation of women in nontraditional roles and occupations. Those who might deny such participation can argue that while it is not naturally determined that women are ill suited to the role of warrior, it is nonetheless true that they are ill suited as a result of their socialization concerning what is appropriate for girls and boys, women and men. Those who support participation can argue that even though some women may be ill suited, others may be quite well suited because they have chosen not to accept the gender limitations that society has tried to place on them. Thus, a social constructionist perspective can be used to the advantage of those on either side of the issue.

The focus here is not to address the "nature/nurture" debate or to weigh in with a definitive response to the various arguments. There are many disparate reasons for the resistance to women taking on roles as warriors. While we come to view those in resistance as sharing a common goal, the justifications for their positions may be quite varied.

Femininity and Masculinity

When a given occupational role is defined as masculine, many automatically challenge women's ability or suitability to assume that role. In a society where we either fail to acknowledge traits in women that seem masculine or censure them, women who seek to enter a work role that is defined as masculine are faced with a number of barriers to their participation.[1] Women may be seen as deviant, and they may find that they have to work at creating an image that allows them to balance their sex-defined gender role with the gendered occupational role.

The concepts of "feminine" and "masculine" are difficult to clarify. They have different meanings for everyone. In my research I chose not to provide respondents with *my* definitions, but, rather, depended on them to define these concepts in their own terms. When asked to define "feminine" and "masculine," respondents generally provided lists of stereotypical characteristics, both positive and negative. It was clear from marginal comments that providing such a definition was problematic for many. A fair number of respondents gave stereotypical responses and then qualified them by noting that while these were "society's definitions," they did not agree. Although some may have trouble defining the concepts, we do seem to be familiar enough with "social definitions" to use them in our daily lives. Few respondents had trouble with the items "I would describe myself as feminine" and "I would describe myself as masculine." Fewer still had trouble answering the multitude of questions about the roles of femininity and masculinity in the participation of women in the military. It seemed that they know how *others* define them, and they have very clear ideas about how one's identification, by others, as feminine or masculine may affect one's participation.

Femininity carries with it both positive and negative connotations; which of these connotations applies varies with the role or situation. In the military, women face ongoing battles over femininity, which is both valued and devalued, the source of both reward and punishment. This dilemma recalls the early days of women's entry into the military, when, on one hand, femininity was discouraged because it symbolized women's inappropriateness for the role they were filling, while, on the other, it was emphasized as a way of illustrating that women could perform military duties and still be "good women."

Although questioned specifically about penalties, a number of the women I surveyed or interviewed pointed out how femininity could be used to improve one's situation in the military. However, there was almost always a cost that went along with the "benefit." As one respondent noted, "It is a perception that military women who may be 'too feminine' get the 'good,' 'high-visibility' jobs on admirals' or generals' staffs." Yet, at the same time, such women are "looked upon as sex objects" and are "not able to show their brains work."

While, in general, masculinity is more valued than femininity, being perceived as masculine may have negative repercussions for women. Women pointed out the contradictory reaction evoked when they are perceived as masculine. Women "who are perceived as having masculine traits [i.e., aggressiveness, tough discipline, directness] may be called names like 'castrating bitch' but still are generally respected and get the job done."

There are many standards against which our performances are measured. Are we good students, good parents, good citizens, and so on? In contemporary Western society there are generally agreed-upon criteria such as grade-point averages, what our children achieve, and whether or not we break the law, that are used to gauge our "goodness." Aside from the issues of chastity and benevolence, there are other, less often articulated questions that society uses to assess our performance as "good women" and "good men." Though the rules are often more implicit than explicit, we function in a world that constantly reminds us of whether or not we are "good" at fulfilling the expected social role of "woman" or "man."

Much of the world is experiencing a great deal of upheaval over the issue of gender and the appropriateness of certain roles for women and men. To cite one recent, and sensationalized, example, women have gone to war while their husbands remained behind and functioned as single parents. But, for every inroad women have made, there have been long uphill fights, often accompanied by severe backsliding. At the micro level, such resistance has often come in the form of attacks on one's ability to achieve such goals and still be a "good" or "real" woman. Thus, at the center of this war is the issue of gender appropriateness—and, as I argue, its link to sexuality.

Gendered Expectations

I first asked my respondents whether they believe that the military pressures or encourages women to "act feminine" or "act masculine." I asked three separate sets of questions, one on issues concerning femininity, one on masculinity, and a third that combined questions on both to reflect the women's beliefs about pressure overall. Then, I asked whether they believe that there are penalties for being perceived as "too feminine" or "too masculine." Again, I used two sets of questions, one to address femininity, the other masculinity.

There are a number of reasons that we might be interested in who thinks what on this issue. If attitudes vary according to different characteristics, this information may be useful to policymakers and military leadership. Do women in one branch of the military feel more pressure to act feminine or masculine? If so, what might this tell us about that branch's training styles or its ability to create a fair and nonhostile work environment? Does rank affect whether or not one believes that such pressure exists? This knowledge, too, might guide policy, particularly in a training environment. What about sexual orientation? Even with the ban on lesbians and gay men still firmly in place, an examination of the experiences of lesbian and bisexual women can provide a wealth of information about the way gender and sexuality structure women's experiences in the military.

The military could conceivably have reasons for demanding either femininity or masculinity. Because of the masculinized nature of the military, women could be expected to maintain a certain degree of femininity, both to emphasize men's masculinity and to maintain more conservative notions of gender appropriateness. On the other hand, if masculinity is the concept around which notions of soldiering are structured, then all soldiers might be expected to display some degree of masculinity, regardless of sex. So, women might be expected to display both femininity *and* masculinity, a demand that would be certain to not exist for male soldiers. Yet, it is also possible that the most desirable position would be to exhibit little gender at all. If the military sees *both* femininity and masculinity in women as undesirable, then it might exert little pressure in either direction.

The survey contained the following questions: 1) Do you think that the military pressures or encourages women in the military to "act feminine?," and 2) Do you believe that the military pressures or encourages women in the military to "act masculine?" In each case I was interested in whether the respondents felt that the military, as an institution, did anything to pressure or encourage them in a particular direction.

My respondents were almost evenly split over whether the military pressures or encourages women toward either femininity or masculinity, with 51 percent indicating that they believe that the military does not pressure or encourage women to act either feminine or masculine.

When responses to the two questions were examined separately, about one-quarter of the respondents believed that the military pressures or encourages women to "act feminine." One-third believed that the military pressures or encourages women to "act masculine." Interestingly, most who believed that such pressures existed believed that they operated only in one direction or the other. Only 10 percent believed there were pressures in both directions.

In order to determine which characteristics might most influence attitudes about whether the military pressures women to act feminine or to act masculine, I used statistical models that allowed me to examine the effects of different characteristics. These characteristics were branch, rank, and sexual orientation.

Popular culture among both current and former military, and to some degree among civilians, tells us that there are significant differences among the different branches of the military. The Air Force, the youngest branch, is viewed as highly technical, as requiring more brains than brawn, and as the least antagonistic to women.[2] The Air Force also has a slightly higher proportion of women. A number of respondents mentioned, without prompting, that having served in the Air

Force might be an important factor in their particular experience. For example, "The military—*especially* the Air Force—was the leader in equal pay and equal opportunity for equal work, in the total labor force!" The Navy, until quite recently, has had the largest share of negative publicity around issues of gender and sexuality. Whether because of the Tailhook scandal of the early 1990s, the chaining of a female midshipman (*sic*) to a urinal at the Naval Academy, or the purging of alleged lesbians aboard ship, the Navy is believed by many to be the branch most antagonistic toward women. The Army and the Marine Corps have traditionally fallen somewhere in the middle. The Army does not have the technical image of the Air Force, nor, until the recent sexual harassment scandal, has it had as problem-ridden an image as the Navy. As the largest branch, it may have escaped a single label. The Marine Corps, the smallest of the branches, is somewhat different from the other three branches. Women in the Marine Corps are, specifically, Women Marines—that is, women first, Marines second. As one woman who agrees with this characterization wrote, "At the time I joined the military the mission of the woman Marine was 'to free a man to fight.' That currently is no longer the policy and I feel it should be. Women and men were created differently." Christine Williams has illustrated the unique position of the woman Marine in her study of women Marines and male nurses. She quotes one respondent as saying:

> A Woman Marine maintains her femininity, her identity as a woman, while also developing that bearing and everything else that goes into being a marine, without losing her feminine, personal image. (1989: 74)

Evidence of the value placed on this feminine image is the fact that, until quite recently, women recruits in the Marine Corps were required to attend makeup and etiquette classes as part of their training. All of this demonstrates that it would be reasonable to assume that attitudes toward women vary among the various branches of the military.

But, when I examined pressure overall, I found that there is no significant difference among the branches. The percentage of women who believed that there is pressure to act either feminine or masculine varied from 41 percent in the Air Force to 56 percent in the Marine Corps, a range of less than 20 percent.

When questions of pressure to act feminine and pressure to act masculine were separated out, the responses were telling. Regarding pressure to act feminine, there was no significant difference between branches. It is on the question of masculinity that there were discrepancies. More than half of the Marines indicated that they believed that the military pressured them to act masculine. This is interesting given that, as discussed earlier, there is a prevalent belief that the Marine Corps works to insure that Women Marines are, in fact, women first. Although statistically significant, these results must be eyed with caution, as the sample contains only eleven Marines. The Army and the Navy are quite close, with a little more than one-third of the women believing that such pressures exist in these branches of the military. Last, one-fifth of Air Force women believe this pressure to exist. When examining these effects in a model that compares the Air Force to the other three branches, I found that a member of the Air Force is significantly more likely to believe that there is little to no pressure to act masculine. These findings are consistent with popular beliefs that the Air Force has integrated women most successfully.

If we can say, with some degree of certainty, that the Air Force has, in fact, been more successful at integrating women, we must ask why and how? Does the fact that the Air Force emphasizes "brains over brawn" really have something to do with it? That is, does the emphasis on technical skill rather than brute strength change the tenor of the organization? Or, is self-selection involved? Are men who are drawn more to a technical setting than to a more physically demanding setting less likely to resist women's participation? I suspect that it is a little of both. Answers to these questions would not only inform military policy regarding how best to address the inclusion of women but might also inform our theoretical understanding of the link between masculinity and occupational choices, including the military.

Any research on the military must take rank into account. Analysis by rank, however, has some unique problems. There are two coexisting rank structures within the military, enlisted and officer. All officers technically outrank all enlisted personnel. However, a hierarchy of junior enlisted through senior enlisted and continuing up through the officer ranks may be misleading. Almost to a person, senior enlisted personnel have spent more time in the service, held more supervisory positions, and become more entrenched in the system than have junior officers, especially those who were not enlisted prior to being commissioned.

I found significant differences according to rank when rank was measured by junior or senior status, regardless of enlisted or officer status. Junior personnel were more likely to believe that overall pressures existed. There were no statistically significant differences when I looked at pressure to act feminine. But, when I asked about the relationship between rank and pressure to act masculine, I found that twice as many junior personnel believed that such pressures existed. When I examined the relationship between "pressure to act masculine" and junior/senior status but controlled for the effect of other characteristics, I found that junior personnel remained more likely to believe that there are pressures to act masculine.

Almost three-quarters of lesbian and bisexual women believed that some type of pressure to act masculine or feminine exists, while 40 percent of heterosexual women thought so. On the question of pressure to act feminine, half of lesbian and bisexual women thought that such pressure existed, while only 17 percent of heterosexual women thought so. Looking at pressure to act masculine, 37 percent of lesbian and bisexual women thought that such pressures existed, while 32 percent of heterosexual women thought so, though this difference was not statistically significant.

Whether looking at pressures to act feminine or pressures to act masculine, when the effect of other characteristics was controlled, my respondents' sexual orientation remained an important factor in determining their responses. While the majority of women did not think such pressures exist, the degree to which this is so differed significantly by sexual orientation. Although the data do not provide an answer to why this is so, I believe that one possibility is that gender issues are more salient for lesbian and bisexual women. In addition, women who indicated that they would describe themselves as masculine were more likely to say that there was pressure to act feminine.

Overall, the findings concerning pressure on women in the military to "act feminine" or "act masculine" are mixed. The question as framed may have left too much room for interpretation. Did the respondents interpret "military" in a narrow, institutional sense, or did they interpret it in terms of daily acts by their superiors and coworkers? While I am not convinced that it makes a difference (to some degree, pressure may be pressure regardless of the source), it makes it difficult to apply any one story to the findings. Overall, while a slight majority (51 percent) of women *do not* think such pressures exist, the 49 percent who do think so constitute a considerable minority. One-quarter (26 percent) of all respondents think there are pressures to act feminine, and one-third (33 percent) think there are pressures to act masculine.

What does it mean if half of one's "employees" believe that they are pressured to act in accordance with a particular set of ideas about gender-appropriate characteristics? From an organizational efficiency perspective, one could argue that time and energy that could otherwise be devoted to the job may be siphoned off for impression management. This can lead to decreased performance and efficiency on the part of those employees. Social psychological interpretations would likely emphasize the costs of not fitting in; employees may experience undue stress and any of the many problems associated with it (e.g., poor physical health, emotional difficulties, substance abuse).

With regard to women in the military, I believe that both analyses have elements of truth. This is to say not that the women don't do their jobs as well as their male counterparts but that they may kill themselves trying. Think of how much better people would perform if they could focus only on the task at hand and not on what their body language might be saying, whether they were being too aggressive or too "laid back," and so on. If these women could just be themselves, there is little doubt that we would observe a reduction in stress, improved individual performance, and a corresponding increase in unit performance.

Penalties for Gender Violations

The military is an arena that is not only numerically male dominated but ideologically male as well. A fair number of the arguments against the participation of women, and lesbians and gays as well, center on the effect of their presence on male bonding, unit cohesion and, even more telling, the image of the military in the eyes of others.

The debates over the lifting of the ban on lesbians and gays in the military highlight a number of issues important to the subject of women in the military. One of these is the importance of masculinity to the military, as evidenced by the continued focus on gay men in the military. During the 1993 Senate hearings and in the press coverage at that time, lesbians were rarely mentioned. The arguments themselves proved even more illuminating. One argument for not allowing *open* lesbians and gays to serve was that they would ruin the image, the masculine image, of the military in the eyes of both Americans and our allies. Another argument was that potential recruits would no longer be attracted to the military as a place where one would be recognized and rewarded for being a "real man." After all, if gay men could participate, then obviously being a "real man" was no longer a requirement (Glidden 1990). Though the debate over lesbians and gays was not intended to be a lesson in the military's perspective on gender, it unintentionally provided significant information on the importance of masculinity to soldiering.

In an occupation where masculinity represents what it means to be a member of that occupation, what happens when women enter the field? If expectations of gender were not so highly correlated with sex, there would be no problem. But, in a world where gender and sex are conflated, the presence of women in a masculine setting may pose a variety of difficulties. Women may be confronted with contradictory gender expectations. On the one hand, one might expect them to be "feminine" because they are women; on the other hand, one might expect them to be "masculine" because they are filling an occupational role that is defined as masculine.

I argue that women may be penalized for being perceived as too feminine *or* too masculine. There is very little latitude for them when it comes to perceptions of gender. To examine this issue, I asked respondents to indicate whether they believed that penalties exist for women who are perceived as "too feminine." In a separate question, I asked whether they believe that penalties exist for women who are perceived as "too masculine."

Ever since women first entered the military, there have been conflicts over how to manage the fact that they were women. Aside from logistical issues such as barracks and latrines, there has been a great deal of concern over appearance, in terms of women's bodies and apparel. In the 1940s, male uniforms had breast pockets. This created a vexing situation for the military. If, as is usually the case, military leaders sought uniformity, then women's uniforms would have to have breast pockets, too. But, that might bring attention to their breasts! After heavy debate, it was decided that women's uniforms would not have breast pockets (Treadwell 1953). Not highlighting anything remotely sexual was more important than creating uniformity. Given the importance of uniformity to the military culture, this decision is quite telling with regard to their take on women's sexuality!

In the late 1970s and early 1980s, a similar question was raised. Women's work uniforms were designed to have the shirt worn outside the pants, over the waist, hips, and buttocks. Men's shirts were to be tucked into their pants. As the women's uniforms, a different uniform altogether, were phased out, women began purchasing the "male" uniform. Nobody could decide whether the women should wear the shirt outside, thus retaining the style of the old women's uniforms, which covered their waists, hips, and buttocks, *or* whether, since the uniform was identical to the men's (it was the *same* uniform), they should tuck their shirts in. For months the rules changed, with women never quite sure how they should wear their uniforms. Ultimately, the decision was made that women should tuck in their shirts. Ironically, these uniforms were soon replaced by a new camouflage uniform for both women and men that called for both sexes to wear the shirt outside the pants.

One ongoing example of the military's difficulty with women, gender, and appearance is the issue of hair length. Military regulations stipulate that a woman's hair is not to fall beneath the bottom of her collar. Yet, the same regulation states that it "must not be cut so short as to appear masculine." As one respondent wrote, "A female soldier I knew had her hair cut short and was reprimanded because the officer in charge felt it looked like a male hair cut."

Clearly, the military continues to wrestle with notions of what it means to be a woman in the military. The military continues to see femininity as something to be denied or, at the very least, controlled. One mechanism for doing this is to exact penalties against women who are perceived to be "too feminine." Not only would this approach, perhaps, "correct the problem" with the individual, but it would serve as a message to other women. I speculated that a majority of women in the military would, in fact, believe that there are penalties for women who are perceived as "too feminine."

What exactly does the phrase "too feminine" mean to these women? As one woman wrote:

> There were women I met who didn't want to break a nail, get their hands dirty, kill in a wartime situation, who wanted the Farrah Fawcett bouffant hairdo, which was impossible to fit under a hat, who wore jewelry that was out of regulation, etc. It was these behaviors that pissed me off as well as the men. It was these behaviors that fed the female stereotype. . . . To me these behaviors were regarded as "too feminine" and had repercussions. (Enlisted, Air Force, heterosexual)

Another wrote, "If a woman doesn't adopt male mannerisms, she is 'too feminine to be a leader.'" Thus, ideas about what behavior is "too feminine" range from demonstrated or perceived excesses of traditionally feminine behaviors, such as wearing makeup and having manicures, to simply failing to adopt more traditionally male behaviors. Appearing "too feminine" seems to involve issues of clothing and makeup, as well as "bodily" characteristics such as "natural beauty," size, and hairstyle. Later I consider the reactions to women who adopt male mannerisms.

In an article on military culture, Karen Dunivin writes, "the combat, masculine-warrior paradigm is the essence of military culture" (1994: 534). For women, this may pose something of a contradiction. For better or worse, women are often expected, by virtue of the sex-gender connection, to display societal norms of femininity. What is expected when women fill an occupational role whose defining characteristics are inexorably linked with masculinity? Women are faced with having to be "masculine enough" to do the job, but not so "masculine" as to be seen as "less than a woman."[3] While women have to fill a masculine work role, it is quite possible that they are also penalized for being "too masculine," for, in essence, violating the societal expectations that they maintain some degree of femininity.

When considering the issue of what constitutes "too masculine," one woman wrote:

> Women who attempt to exercise authority are often seen as too masculine and are penalized by not being given positions of authority in the chain of command. If a woman is naturally assertive and forward it is often an affront to older commanders. (First Lieutenant, Air Force, heterosexual)

Another wrote:

Male officers, who have very traditional ideas (and often misogynistic ones) about women, are irritated and disgusted by women who work on airplanes, which is perceived by many of them as being a masculine duty. (Enlisted, Navy, heterosexual)

The characteristics most frequently associated with being too masculine are aggressiveness and assertiveness, the very qualities that the military sees as desirable in male soldiers, even those not in leadership positions. Some have argued that the military does not desire assertiveness in junior personnel. I disagree; in fact, all soldiers are viewed as potential leaders, as well as followers, from the moment they arrive in basic training. Assertiveness is viewed as desirable when used in the appropriate fashion.

Some women are judged as too masculine simply because they do the very job to which they have been assigned. In general, whether as the result of a personal characteristic or a work-role demand, it seems that doing one's job and doing it well may automatically lead to one's being characterized as masculine. Given the masculine culture of the military, this is not surprising. What is peculiar is a situation where women are penalized for possessing those characteristics seen as highly desirable in male personnel. Yet, this is exactly what happens.

A majority of the women I surveyed believe that there are penalties for being perceived as either "too masculine" (60 percent) or "too feminine" (64 percent), while about half (49 percent) feel that there are penalties for perceived excesses in both directions. That is, not everyone who saw penalties in one case saw them in the other, but half of the sample did believe that violating gender norms in either direction results in penalties.

There are significant differences by branch when the relationship between branch and penalties for femininity is examined. Of the Army women in my study, almost three-quarters believe that there are penalties for being perceived as too feminine. They are followed by the Marine Corps (64 percent), the Navy (56 percent), and the Air Force (53 percent). Just as Air Force women are less likely to perceive pressures to act feminine, Air Force women are also less likely to believe that penalties exist for women who are perceived to be too feminine.

Army women (66 percent) are also those most likely to indicate that the military penalizes women for being "too masculine." They are followed closely by women in the Navy (64 percent). Fifty percent of the Air Force women respondents believe that such penalties exist, while only 40 percent of Marines think so. The latter is consistent with findings that Marines appear more likely to believe that the military pressures them to "act masculine."

The findings regarding penalties for femininity or masculinity by enlisted/officer status are significant only when the effects of other characteristics are controlled. Officers were more likely to see penalties for femininity and slightly more likely to see penalties for masculinity. When I considered junior against senior rank, I found that junior personnel were more likely to believe that penalties of both types existed. Of all junior personnel, almost three-quarters believed that there are penalties for femininity. Just over half of all senior personnel did so. Two-thirds of junior personnel believed that there are penalties for masculinity, compared to just over half of senior personnel. While this appears to be a contradiction, given our tendency to think of junior personnel as enlisted and senior personnel as officers, it is not. The sample contained a great many junior officers whose experiences as both junior personnel and officers contributed to this finding.

When I looked only at the descriptive data, I found that lesbian and bisexual women appeared more likely than heterosexual women to believe that penalties exist for women who are perceived as too feminine. Almost three-quarters of the lesbian and bisexual women surveyed believed such penalties existed, whereas 60 percent of heterosexual women indicated as much. When the data were examined with the the effects of other characteristics controlled for, this relationship disappeared. That is, sexual orientation did not predict whether or not a woman would be more likely to believe that there were penalties for being perceived as too feminine.

Four out of five (81 percent) lesbian and bisexual women felt that penalties existed for women who were perceived as "too masculine," while just over half of heterosexual women indicated as much. When I controlled for the effects of other characteristics, I found that sexual orientation continued to serve as a predictor of whether one believed that there were penalties for being perceived as too masculine.

Lesbian and bisexual women are far more likely to be sensitive to the possibility that women are penalized for being perceived as too masculine. Again, I suspect that gender issues are more salient for lesbian and bisexual women. Given the link between gender and attribution of sexuality, there are good reasons for this heightened level of awareness.

Other characteristics that provided information about who thinks what include race, the year a woman left active duty, and a woman's civilian education at the time she entered the service. Women of color, women who left active duty more recently, and women who began their military careers with less education were more likely to believe that there were penalties for femininity.

Although these data do not provide explanations for these effects, one can speculate. Women of color may be targeted for differential treatment. They are recognized as "other" by virtue of both sex and race. As such, they may truly experience greater pressures to conform to traditional gender expectations. But, it is also important to bear in mind that the number of women of color in the sample was low (28), and this finding might have been different had there been more women of color in the study.

Women who left the military recently are more likely to have experienced a military that was less tolerant of femininity than are women who left the military at earlier times. I suspect that women who served in the past were expected, to some degree, to be a bit more feminine. While they may still have experienced penalties for a perceived excess of femininity, these may have been less severe than the penalties observed by women who served more recently. There is also the possibility that the penalties have actually increased as the numbers of women in the military have risen and a backlash of sorts has occurred.

Finally, women with less education may be more likely to be in areas where there is less tolerance for femininity. Those with more education would be more likely to be in fields such as nursing and military intelligence. Many respondents commented that they thought that they had experienced less harassment, because they were in those fields. For example:

> I was in military intelligence and I believe that if I had served in a different area my experiences would have been worse. I believe that individuals in "MI" are more educated and therefore more amenable to different "lifestyles" and perhaps new ideas in general. (Noncommissioned officer, Army, lesbian)

Although the statistical model controls for the effects of occupation and rank (which are also indicative of education), there are many subtle differences in occupation for which I could not control.

The longer a woman had spent in the military, the less likely she was to believe that penalties exist for femininity. Perhaps women who have stayed in the military have not encountered the same penalties or general problems that led other women to leave the service. It is also quite possible and, I argue, likely that women not only learn how to "get along" but that they become immersed in the system to the point where they do not identify problems in the same fashion as those with less experience. This is partly evidenced by the qualitative data in which women mention how they had to learn how "to deal" with the unpleasantries of military life. None of the other characteristics were significant in predicting beliefs about penalties for masculinity.

Summary

In this chapter I have examined whether women believe that the military pressures or encourages women to "act feminine" or to "act masculine" and whether women believe that there are penalties for being perceived as "too feminine" or "too masculine." I also examined which women are more likely to perceive such pressures and penalties. The results are mixed, but they allow us to draw some general conclusions about the role of gender in the military as it is perceived by the women in this sample.

When examining pressure overall, a significant minority (49 percent) believe that women are pressured or encouraged to act either feminine or masculine. A little more than one-quarter of women see only pressure to act feminine, while one-third of the women believe that there are pressures to act masculine. Thus, while most women do not believe that such pressures exist, enough women do recognize such pressures that the possibility is worth further consideration.

The groups most likely to identify pressure to act feminine were those who described themselves as masculine and those who identified as lesbian and bisexual. Both of these findings conform to what we might expect in any setting where gender is salient and stereotypes prevalent. If they are examined separately, it is perfectly logical to conclude that if a woman sees herself as possessing an attribute (i.e., masculinity) that is not desirable (i.e., in women), she might believe that there are pressures to act in other ways, in this case feminine. Given the stereotypes surrounding lesbians, and to a lesser degree, bisexual women, it is also not surprising that they would be more likely to believe that such pressures exist. As I discuss in chapter 4, women who are considered "too masculine" are also likely to be labeled as lesbians. It is also true that women who are identified as lesbians are assumed by many to be more masculine, regardless of appearance. Again, if masculinity in women is negatively sanctioned, it should not surprise us that these women believe that pressures exist to "act feminine."

Finally, when I looked only at pressures to act masculine, the effect of branch of the military is strong throughout. Women in the Air Force, when compared to women in other branches, are less likely believe that pressures exist to "act masculine." This is consistent with the popular perception of the Air Force as having a more technical orientation than the other branches. Junior women, regardless of branch, are more likely to believe that there are pressures to act masculine. It is quite possible that junior women, even when age, time in service, and other factors are controlled for, feel more pressure to fit the social stereotype of "the soldier," or to prove themselves.

Distinct from the question of pressure is that of penalties. Do women believe that they are penalized for being perceived as "too feminine" or "too masculine"? Findings indicate that more than 60 percent of women believe that penalties exist for either femininity or masculinity. Those with more time in the service are less likely to believe that penalties exist for femininity. Lesbian and bisexual women and junior women, particularly, it seems, junior officers, are more likely to believe that penalties exist for transgressing the boundaries of gender. Not surprisingly, women in the Air Force are less likely, when compared to women in all other branches, to believe that women are penalized for being "too feminine" or "too masculine." It appears that women in the Air Force, when compared to those in all other branches, are far less concerned about pressures or penalties around gender.

The findings presented in this chapter should be viewed as providing a foundation for the questions that are at the heart of this research, namely, whether women strategize around gender in their daily lives and, if so, what types of strategies they employ. It is evident that gender plays a significant role in the experiences of women in the military. What are the penalties for gender deviation? The answer to this question not only illustrates how gender is enforced but reveals, in part, how the construction of sexuality is used as a mechanism for the enforcement of gender.

3

DYKES OR WHORES

Sexuality and the Military

[On the] 2nd day of bootcamp—company commander said, "Welcome to the fleet. In the Navy's eyes you're either dykes or whores—get used to it.

—Noncommissioned officer, Navy, lesbian

The Meaning of Sexuality

Sexuality is a topic that is taboo, yet frequently discussed; concealed, yet present throughout daily life. It can be used as a source of reward or punishment; the expression of sexuality is both demanded and condemned. So all-encompassing is its breadth that it is impossible to provide even a modest social history of sexuality within this text. Rather, I discuss how I use the term "sexuality" and the problems of identifying any true meaning of the term.

Various sources define sexuality as one's "concern with or interest in sexual activity" or "the quality of having a sexual character or potency" (e.g., Webster's, second edition, or the New Riverside University Dictionary). To acknowledge "one's sexuality," especially in recent years, has often meant to acknowledge one's sexual orientation. But, concern with or interest in sexuality is by no means limited to that arena. One's interests in sexuality may be that one prefers "vanilla sex," that one prefers to engage in sex with a variety of partners, or that one is sexually aroused by particular objects; the possibilities are endless. Thus, "sexuality" can be used to describe a broad range of erotic desires, or the lack thereof.

Sexuality can also be used to describe less readily identified aspects of a person. Although assessments of one's sexuality are frequently made by others, they are often made in the absence of any concrete information. That is, it is not unusual for someone to be described in sexual terms, such as "she's hot" or "he's a real stud," when the speaker hasn't the vaguest notion of what the individual is really like sexually. Such characterizations are often made on the basis of appearance and, specifically, on the basis of whether the individual fits very gendered notions of what is appealing. Thus, one's sexuality can be viewed as an amalgamation of one's sexual interests and the degree to which one exhibits those interests, whether through one's own actions or in the judgment of those around one. It is this definition that best describes the way I use the term "sexuality" in this research.

It is not possible to provide a sweeping description of the meaning of sexuality, even when confining our discussion to contemporary Western societies. As has been noted, "sexual meanings are not universal absolutes, but ambiguous and problematic categories" (Plummer 1982: 231). Jeffrey Weeks, in his book titled simply *Sexuality*, has discussed the importance of clarifying the meaning, or meanings, of sexuality. He writes, "This is an easy aim to proclaim. It is a notoriously more hazardous task to carry out" (1986: 12). How we describe, perceive, or enact sexuality varies on any number of dimensions— class, race, religion, education, and so forth. And, if we were to identify some shared understanding of sexuality, the fluidity of the concept would leave us questioning that understanding only moments after we articulated it. Sexuality and its meaning seem to lie in something of a poststructuralist Pandora's box. What it means to the individual or the collective today may not hold true tomorrow. Thus, articulating any "true meaning" of sexuality is a daunting task.

What, then, can be said about the meaning of sexuality at all? For some, it is something to be kept hidden, to be discussed only when absolutely necessary, such as in what some experience as wedding-eve talks between mother and daughter. For others, sexuality is publicly proclaimed, as in the wearing of a t-shirt that reads, "Nobody Knows I'm A Lesbian." These examples are reflections of social attitudes toward sexuality in that many would describe sexuality as either very private or exceedingly public. As such, they illustrate the problem of developing a shared meaning of sexuality. Yet, they also illustrate the falsity of the notion that sexuality is, at any level, solely private.

The ritual of the wedding[1] is itself a public statement about one's sexuality, though it is rarely acknowledged as such. It suggests that one a) is heterosexual and b) intends to engage in sexual activity. While the determination of these "facts" may be made in error (i.e., the participants may not be heterosexual and/or may not intend to engage in sexual activity), the truth is that most people would agree that these are the assumptions one makes when they see or hear that someone is marrying. Thus, social, cultural, and legal facts about marriage allow us to draw conclusions about sexuality from a relatively "nonsexual" ritual. While the personal meaning of sexuality may vary, there should be little doubt about the degree to which sexuality permeates the public sphere.

In teaching about gender and sexuality, I find that students are often at a loss to see the extent to which sex is used in advertising or rock videos. Many people accuse gays and lesbians of "flaunting it," yet fail to see the degree to which heterosexuality is "flaunted" each and every day. The normative status granted to heterosexuality renders its dominance invisible.

Femininity, Masculinity, and Sexuality

"One of the primary ways in which cultural values permeate notions of gender is, of course, in the approach to sexuality . . ." (Siann 1994: 10) That is, any meaning granted to sexuality varies not only between women and men as individuals but between women and men as categories of people. The cliché "Men need sex to have love, women need love to have sex," suggests the cultural attitudes that surround gender and sexuality.

I have discussed the way that gender is viewed by some as "naturally" derived from one's status as female or male. I also indicated that, in much of the scholarship on gender, this perspective has taken a backseat to the belief that gender is socially created. Such is not the case with sexuality. "At no point is the belief in the natural and universal human more entrenched than in the study of sexuality" (Gagnon and Simon 1973: 3–4). Because we see sexuality as being primarily a result of our biology (i.e., our being female or male), the tendency has been to view sexuality as something defined in terms of nature and, thus, as clearly defined and unchanging. This position has been under assault, but it is not about to disappear.

We are presented with parallel beliefs about gender and sexuality. These beliefs are that gender (i.e., displaying femininity and/or masculinity) and sexuality, as previously defined, are naturally derived and unchanging. Such a perspective also implies, by definition, that any sexual behavior that is perceived as less than natural is, in fact, unnatural. Each set of beliefs (i.e., toward gender or sexuality) could, theoretically, exist without the other. Yet, in reality, what we observe is the conflation of gender and sexuality, made even easier by the belief that both gender and sexuality are expressions of something inherently natural in origin. The critical link between the two, and one of the major underpinnings of this research, is that each reinforces the other.

How do "gender rules," or what is considered appropriate for women and men, intersect with sexuality? We learn at a young age what it means to be a girl or a boy, not in terms of sex organs, but in terms of femininity and masculinity. One of the mechanisms by which society enforces these rules is to suggest that when one's "gender" does not correspond with one's "sex," the individual must be homosexual. There is a tendency to conflate gender with sexuality so that while normative patterns of gender (e.g., the exhibition by men of appropriate masculinity) lead to assumptions of heterosexuality, gender nonconformity (e.g., failure by men to exhibit masculinity appropriately *or* their exhibition of femininity) suggests homosexuality. Thus, women who engage in behaviors that are viewed as gender nonconforming, such as joining the military, may have their sexuality questioned on the basis of that act alone.

The link between gender and sexuality is also highly visible when the topic is not sexual orientation but sexual behavior in general. Consider, for example, the way in which women and men are characterized when the subject is "promiscuity." Depending on the setting, women are both feminized and defeminized as a result of their sexual behavior, real or imagined. In one instance, the sexually available woman (e.g., the mistress) may be highly feminized. In another, she may be viewed as masculinized (e.g., the woman who initiates sex). A man who has, or is believed to have, numerous sexual encounters may be highly masculinized (e.g., the stud). The man who is perceived, accurately or not, to have limited sexual experience may be feminized (e.g., Mama's boy). The relationship between gender and sexuality is complex, with ideas about one serving to reinforce the other.

The use of sexuality (i.e., the threat of deviant labels—slut, whore, homosexual) to enforce gender rules is the more obvious side of the relationship. To insure that "girls act like girls and boys like boys," they are threatened with labels that question their sexual behavior. But, in the dialectic of sexuality and gender, gender rules are also used to enforce sexuality. When a female is called "butch," or a male "prissy," that is, when gender display is seen as inconsistent with physiological sex, the underlying message is often that in violating gender rules one is looking or acting "like a homosexual"—and is obviously not a "real" woman or man.

In military training, men are often called "girl," "pussy," or "skirt." To be "feminized" is a mechanism for making men desperate to become "real men." In the case of military training, it is not so much a matter of not following "gender rules" but of not being man "enough" to be a soldier. It may seem that to assert that there are two directions of enforcement (i.e, sexuality to enforce gender and gender to enforce sexuality) is splitting hairs. But, it is worth clarifying that in some instances, it is clearly sexuality that is being negatively sanctioned, while in others it is gender, or femininity or masculinity.

The Sexualization of the Workplace

In an essay on sociology and sexuality, the sociologist Steven Epstein asks two important questions: 1) "How do gender and sexuality structure the shop-floor relations between workers and management, and how do such relations in turn affect patterns of gender and sexuality?" and 2) "Which institutions are central to the reproduction or contestation of sexual codes and beliefs?" (1994: 198–199). Both questions are vital to any research that seeks to address the role of sexuality in the public sphere. It is only recently that scholars have begun to consider the possibility that sexuality does, in fact, structure anything beyond intimate relationships.

Most people would likely agree with statements such as "there is no place for sex in the workplace" and "sexuality should be kept private." A striking illustration of our confusion over sex, sexuality, and sexual orientation is the fact that many lesbians and gay men do not feel it is appropriate to mention their same-sex partners in the office, while discussion of other-sex partners is both expected and encouraged. Homophobia aside, the illustrative aspect of this example is the way in which the same behaviors (e.g., dating, sex, and commitment) take on different meanings depending upon whether or not they are viewed as normative behaviors. The real question is not whether sexuality is or should be "private" but what *types* of sexuality are expected to be kept private. As in the case of the wedding, social life is filled with situations in which sexuality is made public; yet a wedding, for example, is so public, so commonplace, that we fail to see it as sexuality, or an indicator of sexuality, at all.

While most "public sexuality" implies heterosexuality, sexual orientation is not the only issue to be highlighted. Also in question are issues such as sexual interests (e.g., do you laugh at sexual jokes?) or sexual availability (e.g., are you single?) in general. The reason it is impossible to discuss these without reference to sexual orientation is that virtually every aspect of sexuality includes the expectation that all sexuality is heterosexual.

Many people don't recognize the degree to which the public sphere, in this case the workplace, is sexualized. This is partly due to what I call the "invisibility" of heterosexuality. In an ironic twist, by being so dominant a part of social organization, it becomes, in a sense, invisible. Our inability to see the workplace as sexualized is also due to the histories of work (in the public domain) and sexuality. Drawing heavily on Max Weber, James Woods reminds us:

> We imagine that work is a rational activity and that workplaces depend on order. Sexuality, in contrast, is perceived as a threat to all that is rational and ordered, the antithesis of organization. (1993: 33)

Given the lengthy association of work with rationality and the even longer history of sexuality as lustful irrationality, one should not be surprised that a culture has emerged in which they are viewed as diametrically opposed. Sexuality in the workplace is seen not as an inherent part of the social organization of work but rather as an intruder into a space perceived as both rational and asexual.

But, think for a moment about the many persons who place family photos on their desks, who wear wedding or engagement rings; the office parties celebrating engagements, marriages, births, and other personal events; "family picnics"; office chatter; and institutional benefits (e.g, medical insurance, tuition reimbursement, survivor's benefits) All provide clues to one's sexual identity and, often, behavior. But, there are many other ways in which sexuality is made even more explicit. Think about office romances, matchmaking, and the many other ways in which sexuality is suggested in the workplace. "Sexuality is alluded to in dress and self-presentation, in jokes and gossip, in looks and flirtations . . . " (Woods 1993: 22). It becomes difficult to imagine a workplace in which all hints of sexuality are obscured. The role of sexuality in the workplace is undeniable. What is now called for is an understanding of that role, specifically of the way sexuality structures social interaction, at both the interpersonal and the institutional levels.

The military is the ideal setting in which to observe hierarchy, order, and bureaucracy. It appears to be the archetype of both asexuality and rationality, thus sitting in radical opposition to sexuality. But, in fact, sexuality has always been a part of the military, whether formally or informally. There exist numerous accounts of the military's use of sexuality as a mechanism of control over its own troops as well as those around them (Enloe 1989, 1993). Historically, in many instances prostitution was organized, or at the very least made available, by the military. As was discussed in chapter 1, proclamations of sexual prowess have long served as "proof" of masculinity. Yet, the type of sexuality has been regulated as well. And, this regulation is not solely with regard to sexual orientation. There is an old military saying: "If the Army wanted you to have a wife, they would have issued you one." "Occasional satisfaction of sexual desire with a prostitute is okay, but don't saddle yourself with a wife," seemed to be the message.

As should be evident by now, there are many ways of thinking about sexuality and an equal number of ways of thinking about the sexualization of the workplace. The discussion thus far should raise questions not about whether or not sexuality is present in the public sphere (it clearly is); rather, questions should arise over how sexuality shapes our experiences in the public sphere. How is sexuality used to regulate our actions, specifically with regard to gender? How can sexuality, or attributions of sexuality, be used as a source of reward and punishment?

Sexuality and the Enforcement of Gender

Close to two-thirds of the women in my study answered affirmatively to the question of whether women were penalized when they were perceived to be "too feminine." Six general categories of penalty emerged from the women's reports. They are:

1. Being ostracized or disapproved of by other women
2. Being viewed as a slut or sexually available
3. Being perceived as weak
4. Being perceived as incompetent or incapable
5. Not being taken seriously
6. Being limited in career mobility

While it might be argued that some of these categories overlap or are even the same (e.g., weak vs. incompetent), the specific words were used enough, and often within the same response, that they seemed to have different meanings for the respondents.

One assumption held by many in the general public is that penalties are leveled against women by men. However, women's experiences indicate otherwise. About 12 percent of the women in my study indicated that women who were perceived as too feminine were likely to face ostracism or disapproval by other women. One respondent stated, "Penalties of ostracism from other females, not necessarily [the] chain of command." Some stated specifically that penalties were likely to come from women and men alike. For example, "If [a] female acts too feminine to where she expects someone to help her with her duties then she would be harassed by males and females alike," or "Men and women . . . may see them more as a woman first and a soldier second." In these cases, the penalty itself may be ostracism. In other cases, the penalty may be a more specific form of ostracism or disapproval, but it may still come from other women. Consider the woman who wrote, "The female and male soldiers don't give complete respect. . . ." In this instance, the more specific penalty is lack of respect, but it is not only male soldiers who have used this as the means to express their "disapproval" of femininity.

In some cases, respondents focused specifically on penalties that come from women. Take, for example, the following incident:

> We had a female tech working with us briefly in San Antonio—real sweet, soft spoken, extremely attractive—cute and cuddly! Knew her job and did it very well. But the other female techs hated her—not only was she a girl-girl, but she was respected—those other females actually started a rumor that she was promoted early because of her looks—she, although I asked her not to, requested a new assignment—that happens a lot. (Enlisted, Army, heterosexual)

Another indicated that "if they play little-girl or ingenue to get out of disagreeable tasks, they'll certainly be put off by other military women."

The second penalty is the perception that a feminine woman is a "slut," or sexually available. "Someone who is seen as being too feminine may be 'sexualized' and seen as a sexual object vs. an individual with strengths and capabilities." Some responses in this category made it clear that this was not the writer's opinion, while other respondents clearly shared this view. One woman wrote:

> When I saw a woman in uniform with too much makeup, too-long, painted nails, too high of heels, too tightly dressed—*I was prejudiced.* I felt she made us all look bad. As though all my fight to be seen as a competent, goal oriented officer was denigrated by her obvious *sexual* appearance. (Captain, Army, heterosexual)

Others suggested that women who are perceived as too feminine will be "accused of . . . using sex to get ahead," "looked up[on] as 'easy' meaning eager to have sexual relations with men," or seen as "just want[ing] to get married." One woman indicated that "women who are too feminine are perceived . . . as playthings, as 'fresh meat,'" while another said that "feminine women were sometimes seen as uncommitted or using the Army as a 'dating pool.'"

Here again the general versus specific nature of penalties is clear. One respondent indicated that a woman in her company "was subjected to sexual taunts, come-ons, etc., because she was very pretty and wore makeup." While the explicit penalty is harassment, the more subtle "penalty" appears to be the perception that she might be more receptive to men's advances.

It was clear that women were also likely to be perceived as weak. It often seems that in the military all women are assumed to be weak until proven otherwise. A case in point is Brian Mitchell's diatribe against women in the military, *Weak Link: The Feminization of the American Military* (1989). In his book, all women are described as liabilities to the military, regardless of their gender attributes, though women seen as hyperfeminine are even more likely to be regarded as weak. As one woman in my study wrote, "Femininity is sometimes perceived as weakness by unenlightened males. . . ." Others wrote, "Women who are too feminine are perceived as weak," and, "Thought of as soft, weak, not as qualified to do typical male jobs." The latter is perhaps a good example of the overlap between weakness and the fourth penalty, perceptions that one is incompetent and incapable.

Two respondents wrote, "I think the penalties are that the perception of a woman being 'feminine' is somehow equated to a woman being less capable" and, "Sometimes they are looked at as incompetent in their work fields." Other respondents did not use the words "incompetent" or "incapable" but provided descriptions that could be categorized as such. For example, "Perceived as dumb, ineffectual, a joke," or, "Being too feminine means almost being a useless worker. Guys may like to look at a 'dumb blonde,' but they don't want to do their work and hers, too." "People don't think they [are] tough enough to handle being a soldier and performing their jobs." Women who are perceived as too feminine are viewed as antithetical to the military and, as such, are seen as incapable of performing the jobs that the military requires of them.

Closely related to perceptions of incompetence is a failure to take a woman, or women, seriously. Again, most examples use this language quite explicitly ("Women are not taken as seriously as men"), while others provide less direct descriptions such as "you're perceived as a pushover" and "their opinions matter less." One example illustrates how not being taken seriously, indirectly stated, is closely linked to other penalties such as being sexualized: " . . . men will be checking out the packaging and not the information or commands she's delivering." Another instance highlights the connection between not being taken seriously and the sixth category of penalties, facing career limitations. As one woman noted, "They don't get to compete for promotions, because they are not taken seriously by the 'old boy' network."

All five of the penalties discussed thus far are, no doubt, penalties in and of themselves. Yet, all are related to the sixth and most frequently mentioned penalty, career limitations. This is true almost by definition; if a penalty had no potentially negative impact on one's performance or career aspirations, one might question whether in fact it constituted a penalty. It is difficult to think of a situation in which a woman is penalized that does not carry with it the potential to damage one's work relationships and/or career.

"Limited in career mobility" is actually a catch-all phrase for a number of career penalties. They include, but are certainly not limited to, obvious limitations such as not being allowed to perform the job for which one was trained, not being promoted, not being sent to a school needed for promotion, and not getting choice assignments. "They are not assigned to 'career building' areas such as pilots, maintenance, security police—the generally thought-of 'male jobs.'" Another woman wrote:

> I was a long-haired blonde, outstanding figure, long beautiful nails (my own!), etc., etc. I was constantly told I couldn't do my job (working on aircraft) as I was a dumb blonde, I'd get my nails dirty, I was a danger to the guys working on aircraft because I distracted them, etc.,

etc. My first rating was not a favorable one even though
I scored higher on the OJT [on-the-job-training] tests
than anyone had ever scored in that shop! (Enlisted, Air
Force, heterosexual)

Another woman indicated that "you don't get the tough jobs
you need to be in good shape for promotion, and women who
are too feminine usually get ignored or put in office jobs with
no troops." A command position in which one leads troops is
critical to the continued promotion within the officer ranks.
Many women mentioned the penalty of being "removed from
position[s] of authority and placed in somebody's office," or
being "given more feminine jobs to do." Command positions
are definitely not considered "feminine." One woman expressed her opinion on this issue:

It is a great privilege as an officer to be in a command
position. Part of being a commander is having a "command presence." I greatly doubt that women who wear
lots of perfume, makeup, speak softly, and/or make
strong efforts to appear feminine are considered frequently as serious contenders for command positions.
(First Lieutenant, Army, heterosexual)

Other limitations include being "given more feminine jobs to
do" such as clerk-typist, though this was sometimes portrayed
as both positive and negative: "positive" in that the jobs are
often highly desirable positions with "perks" such as being in-
doors, having regular hours, or working for senior officers,
and "negative" in that they are often seen as requiring little
skill and are often not the jobs for which one was trained. As
one respondent indicated, "They are given cushy positions

and not able to show their brains work." In other cases they mentioned being "considered 'brainless' and given fewer opportunities" and being "good enough for paperwork—not real work or tough decisions."

The significant degree to which each of these categories merges with others should be readily apparent. Especially in a military that "has no place for weakness," it is difficult to discuss attributions of weakness without also discussing incompetence. And, it is difficult to discuss perceptions of incompetence without noting its relationship to not being taken seriously and to suffering career limitations. In sum, while about one-quarter of the women mentioned career limitations explicitly ("Not selected for schools, promotion"), virtually all of the penalties discussed related, directly or indirectly, to the ability of women to be treated as equal to men and, therefore, to achieve the same degree of success as their male counterparts.

These six categories covered almost all of the responses. A few did not quite fit with any of the six, but they did not appear frequently enough to warrant being considered categories on their own. These penalties, which might, in fact, have been force-coded into the six penalties, include: lack of respect, harassment, categorization as an "airhead" or as "ditzy," and a perception that one lacks authority or leadership. Other responses addressed a more general sense of being "picked on" or of just not "fitting in." Consider the woman who wrote:

> It depends on if the woman plays according to the "White Male System" and is competent. If she does both of these, she'll have the best chance; If she is competent, but bucks the "White Male System," she'll have trou-

bles. Sort of like advertising you're a Democrat in the military! (Major, Army, heterosexual)

While the penalties for being perceived as too feminine are varied, they do share a common theme. Whether at the informal (e.g., perceived as a slut by other members of the unit) or formal level (e.g., not being selected to attend leadership training), each penalty serves as a mechanism for insuring that women remain "outsiders" to the boys' club of the military.

These examples illustrate the ways in which femininity is viewed as undesirable. The contradiction between the ideology of soldiering and cultural conceptions of femininity insures that it will be difficult for the two to coexist. It also insures that hyperfemininity, or perceptions thereof, is available as a "marker" for women's difference. In chapter 1 I briefly mentioned the way that the military might prefer that women express femininity. The data provided here do not preclude such a position; nor do they allow us to determine to what extent the military might both prefer, yet negatively sanction, femininity. Regardless of any intent on the part of the institution or the persons who make up that institution, it is clear that, for some women, perceptions of femininity insure that they will not be permitted to participate fully at a level equal to that of their male counterparts.

If women who are perceived as too feminine experience penalties, what happens to those women who are perceived as too masculine? Are they polar opposites on some scale of acceptability? One might argue that the best mechanism for combating penalties for being too feminine is to insure that one is perceived as masculine. But the women's experiences reveal that this is not the case.

Slightly more than half of the respondents indicated that they believed that there were penalties for being perceived as "too masculine." Of the women who described the penalties for being perceived as too masculine, more than half suggested that such women would be labeled lesbians. A number of responses could not be coded as such but seemed to carry a strong implication that this was what the respondent was referring to. Consider these examples: "Comments," "Many lewd remarks were made about 'masculine' type women," "I think they may have to prove themselves more especially if not married," and "'Too masculine' tends to be equated with 'man-hating.'" If descriptions of this type were included, about two-thirds of the responses could be considered to address lesbianism.

Although the label "lesbian" emerges as a single category of penalty, it is illustrative to look at the different ways in which the issue is addressed. In many cases women stated very plainly, "Perceived as being a lesbian," "Perceived as lesbians," "Lesbo, dyke, etc.—Need I say more!" In other cases, their descriptions were much more colorful or detailed. Consider the following description:

> Being teased by other servicemembers . . . called "butch," "bitch," "dyke," a lesbian. If a female can't be told apart visually, at first glance, from a male she *will* be subjected to being called sir vs. ma'am and may be kicked out of a few female restrooms, at first glance. (Noncommissioned officer, Navy, heterosexual)

A number of respondents indicated that penalties sometimes came from other women, as was the case for women who were perceived as too feminine. One woman wrote:

> If you go past gender-neutral (the "ideal" woman officer), past masculine (conspicuous), to too masculine, you were courting being labeled a lesbian. Too masculine made men and women nervous. Me, too. (Lieutenant JG, Navy, heterosexual)

Another respondent indicated that "they are often avoided by both male and female soldiers. They are the outcasts of the unit."

One of the most revealing findings regarding the penalty of being labeled a lesbian is the understanding that this label was often applied to women regardless of their sexual orientation. This fact serves as a wonderful illustration of the way in which homophobia and perceptions of sexual orientation serve as mechanisms for the subjugation of all women. "I believe they are labeled as homosexuals, 'dykes,' whether they are or not." "Of course, they are tagged or stereotyped as lesbians, whether they are or not." The impact of such allegations can extend well beyond having to tolerate "talk." As one woman wrote:

> One of the women in the unit who had a masculine appearance was accused of being a lesbian even though she wasn't. When her time was up she got out because of the accusations she was gay. She was a good soldier. (Noncommissioned officer, Army, lesbian)

Being labeled a lesbian was the penalty most frequently cited by the women. Other penalties that respondents described included: 1) ostracism and ridicule and 2) career limitations. Though each of these penalties was cited in only about 10 percent of the women's descriptions, it is important to address them for in these "nonsexualized" instances, women endured social and career penalties for exhibiting behavior that is highly desirable in male service members. It is critical to understand that women are being penalized for exhibiting gendered behaviors that are consistent with the work role of "soldier."

Bearing in mind that we are talking about the military, consider this description of how, and for what, women are penalized. "Women who were seen as too aggressive—too much focus on aggressive or violent activities—were not seen as 'normal' or to be 'trusted.'" Exhibiting interests in activities that many would agree form the core of military ideology (i.e., aggression and violence) results in the penalty of not being considered "normal" or "trustworthy." Another respondent wrote that "women were discouraged from being aggressive, displaying leadership skills, being self-assured and independent."

The ostracism that women describe is often, but not always, linked to the subject of lesbianism. While some women offered descriptions such as, "They are shunned, called names (e.g., dyke)," others were less specific in their remarks, noting only "Rejected by both male and female peers" or "A woman who appears too masculine may be ridiculed for it." One woman wrote, "Yeah, everybody hates them." Whether or not explicitly related to sexual orientation, it is apparent that women who violate gender norms by being too masculine are "outsiders" to the same degree, albeit in a different fashion, as

women who violate the masculine work role of the military by
being too feminine.

By understanding that women receive career penalties for
being perceived as too masculine, as well as for appearing too
feminine, we begin to understand the degree to which women
are required to walk a fine line. Women may be penalized for
possessing qualities that are desirable in military men (e.g., assertiveness, aggression). One woman's comments capture this
contradiction beautifully:

> [I] knew a female airman [*sic*] who could do her job on
> the flight line better than most of the guys in her unit.
> This convinced some people she was a "dyke"— just
> had to be a lesbian otherwise she wouldn't have been so
> good at a "man's job." (Captain, Air Force, heterosex-
> ual)

Although cast in the light of sexual orientation, such a description illustrates the difficulties women face when simply
trying to do the job for which they were recruited. Another
wrote:

> A female commander who does the exact same discipline
> as a male commander is probably seen as a bitch on a
> power trip. You're derided and not respected for playing
> tough by the rules. . . . You play by their rules but then
> you lose because they didn't consider you part of their
> game. (Captain, Army, lesbian)

In other instances, the examples described specific career
penalties, such as "not selected for 'high-profile' jobs,"
"poor evaluations or less than deserved marks," and "over-
looked for awards/promotions." As one woman wrote, "I

believe it can affect performance reviews, assignments, and coaching or counseling which is provided for developmental growth." While the cynic might argue that women "just have to tough it out," it is clear that there are plenty of formal mechanisms by which women can be penalized if they are perceived as gender deviant, regardless of the direction of the alleged deviance.

Summary

In this chapter I have provided descriptions of the penalties that women believe are leveled against those women who are perceived to violate gender norms. While the penalties vary, one major finding is that women are compelled to strike a balance between the "feminine demands" of their sex role and the "masculine demands" of their work role. The other major finding is that both types of gender violations result in attributions of "deviant" sexuality.

It is not surprising that women who are perceived to be too feminine are penalized. Many men perceive the military as a male domain that has been invaded by women. It is femininity that highlights theses "invaders'" status as women and, perhaps more important, their alleged inability to soldier. After all, we, as a society, do not associate femininity with the presumed physical and mental demands of war. If control is to be exerted over the participation of women, what better to focus on than that which many view as an essential aspect of being female?

While women can attempt to combat accusations of weakness, incompetence, or poor performance by insuring that they are so good that they are invulnerable, quashing allegations that one is a slut is much more difficult. Not a few girls and women have been faced with this dilemma. Some would suggest that a woman can "solve" the problem by getting a boyfriend and making certain that everyone knows that she is in a committed relationship. But, what happens when that relationship is terminated? Others would suggest that the best solution is not to date men in one's unit, to insure that they know that one does not engage in sexual activity with these men. Yet, that, too, renders the woman suspect. The truth is that femininity offers no protection against accusations of lesbianism. As some women indicated in their comments about sexual harassment, women who refuse to date or engage in sex with coworkers are often told explicitly that "they must be lesbians." These situations are evidence for the control of women by men as well as for the way in which sexuality intersects with gender to allow such control to occur.

The threat of being labeled a lesbian has been used to intimidate women in a variety of settings. Whether looking at all-female settings such as the convent (Curb and Manahan 1985), civilian occupations (Schneider 1988), or the women's movement (Pharr 1988), researchers find ample evidence to support the assertion that lesbian baiting has often been used to isolate women from one another and to keep them off "male turf." Even the most comprehensive history of the Women's Army Corps cites the use of similar tactics to tarnish the image of military women (Treadwell 1953). More recently, Benecke and Dodge (1996) discussed the role of lesbian baiting in the military not only to eliminate lesbian and bisexual women but also to isolate heterosexual women from one another.

One could argue that the policy against gays and lesbians has proved to be somewhat "functional" for the military, if only in hindsight. By subscribing to stereotypical views of gay men, the military has been able to use homophobia to demand that male recruits show only their strength and their aggression and to insure that those who did not "fit" were totally ostracized by their peers. Although there are many inherent conflicts within such a system,[2] the military has used homophobia, institutional as well as informal, to maintain a myth of masculinity as a prerequisite for service. At the same time, the ban allows the military to eliminate, or at the very least to control, women who, by virtue of fitting the gendered work role of the military, are perceived to violate expected gender roles.

Such a policy and its enforcement may discourage women from entering those jobs that are seen as most masculine, thus allowing the military to preserve some arenas, beyond those already closed to women because of combat restrictions, "for men only." Additionally, it may give the military a way in which to keep women from being "too good," thus guaranteeing that most of the top performers are male. Both of these "benefits" depend to a large degree on the notion that there exists a preferred gender ideology. The ban on lesbians and gay men also keeps women from forming alliances with one another and potentially mobilizing against any perceived injustices. Thus, homophobia interacts with gender ideology to insure that the military remains a predominantly male institution, numerically as well as ideologically.

> If we do gender appropriately, we simultaneously sustain, reproduce, and render legitimate the institutional arrangements that are based on sex category. If we fail to

do gender appropriately, we as individuals—not the institutional arrangements—may be called to account (for our character, motives, and predispositions). (West and Zimmerman 1987: 146)

Even in the wake of incidents like Tailhook and the recent Army sexual harassment cases, it is clear that it is women who are being called to account. Lieutenant Paula Coughlin, the Naval officer who publicized the events at the Tailhook convention, is still being asked why she allowed herself to be present when she "knew" what the parties were like and had, herself, been drinking. Jessica Bleckley, the young woman who first spoke out about her harassment at the Aberdeen Proving Ground and who has since been discharged, continues to be questioned—by the Army, the media, and, no doubt, the public—as to whether she was truthful in her accusations. Just as women have long been held accountable for rape because of their dress, women continue to be held accountable for not "doing gender" appropriately.

4

CAMOUFLAGE ISN'T ONLY FOR COMBAT

> We cannot always be just "feminine" or
> "masculine." I found myself being a combi-
> nation of both at times; it all depends on
> who you're dealing with.
> —Enlisted, Army, heterosexual

Strategies for Gender Management

Women may respond in several ways to the notion that gender has much greater meaning in the workplace than simply
being female or male, "feminine" or "masculine." A woman
may choose to emphasize *either* characteristic, or set of characteristics. Or, she may emphasize *both*, depending on the specific setting in which she is operating at a particular time. In a
military setting, we could tell a convincing story as to why
each one of these might be a likely choice.

Much of the work on the management of gender has focused on professional women or women in business and management (Amatea and Fong-Beyette 1987; Sheppard 1989;
Stivers 1993). While the military contains professional and

managerial positions, it shares as much with vocational and technical occupations as it does with the professions and management. Of course, this varies a good deal by assignment, occupational specialty, and so on. Nonetheless, the environment of the military is quite different from most professional or managerial settings.

In her work on women managers, Deborah L. Sheppard (1989) describes the processes of managing gender. She suggests that women must learn how to "redefine and manage" being female. She writes, "Deliberate behaviours were seen as needed to balance the conflicting statuses of 'female' and 'manager' and such strategies were seen as necessary for organizational success" (1989: 144–145). "Blending," one strategy for managing gender in the organizational setting, "depends on a very careful management of being 'feminine enough' . . . while simultaneously being 'businesslike enough' (. . . in other words, stereotypically masculine)" (Sheppard 1989: 146). Echoing Sheppard, I argue that the difficulty for women in the military is in figuring out how to balance the two competing demands.

Women also need to minimize their sexuality while still maintaining some degree of "femininity." They must strike a balance between femininity and masculinity in which they are feminine enough to be perceived as women, specifically heterosexual women, yet masculine enough to be perceived as capable of soldiering.

One of the contributions of this research is the collection of empirical data on how women "do gender." There is, however, one major difficulty with this type of research: it is based on information that must be recalled by the respondent. For women who have been out of the military for a number of years, it may be difficult to recall and identify strategic behaviors. In addition, there may be an effect of time; women may fail to recall what could be perceived as "negative" aspects of their service. Even when respondents are thinking about more recent events, there is a high likelihood that many behaviors that are forms of strategy are not identified as such. As one woman wrote, "I was too busy doing my job, *as me*, being myself, to worry about artificialities." Another believed that:

> the most successful women were those who didn't worry about being masculine or feminine, but were just themselves, with whatever mix of masculine/feminine attributes they happened to have, and used those attributes to accomplish the mission. (Major, Army, heterosexual)

It is important to note that strategies may not be deliberate or even conscious. Sheppard states:

> A number of women respondents initially stated that gender was not a factor for them at work and that being female was not important. Subsequently they described a variety of strategies including dress, language and relationships with peers and superiors, although they didn't particularly identify them as strategies related to being female. (1989: 145).

Given these constraints, the findings presented here must be viewed as conservative estimates of the degree to which women strategize around gender.

Respondents in this study were given a list of twenty-eight behaviors (See Methodological Appendix, survey items

122–149) and were asked to "check any of the following that you believe applied to yourself" (while on active duty). These items included behaviors such as polishing one's fingernails, wearing cologne on duty, keeping one's hair trimmed above the collar, and socializing with the men in the unit. Respondents were then asked, "Do you believe that any of those behaviors checked in items 122 to 149 were part of a conscious attempt to insure that others perceived you as feminine?" The same question was asked with regard to perceptions as masculine. These items are referred to as closed-ended strategies.

Respondents were also asked the question, "Are there other things that you did that you believe were a conscious attempt to insure that others perceived you as feminine/masculine?" These items are referred to as open-ended strategies. This question was included in the survey because it was impossible to provide a list of all possible strategies. It was likely that there were many things respondents would identify as strategies that would not have occurred to me.

If a respondent indicated that at least one of the twenty-eight closed-ended strategies was part of a conscious attempt to be perceived as feminine or masculine, then that respondent was considered to have employed strategies to manage gender. Forty-two percent, or close to half, of the sample indicated that they engaged in some form of gender management, or strategizing.

When strategizing is examined with regard to femininity *only* or masculinity *only*, slightly fewer than one-third (30 percent) indicated strategizing toward femininity only, while only 6 percent strategized toward masculinity only. Seven percent indicated strategizing in both directions. If we look at those women who engaged in *any* strategizing toward femininity (i.e., "femininity only" and "femininity and masculinity"), we find that slightly more than one-third (37 percent) engaged in strategies of femininity. If we look at those women who engaged in *any* strategizing toward masculinity (i.e., "masculinity only" and "masculinity and femininity"), we find that about one in eight (13 percent) engaged in strategies of masculinity.

The various strategies used to highlight femininity are best viewed as a representation of the whole, rather than as dis-

TABLE 4.1
Distribution of Strategies

Strategies Identified in Closed-Ended Questions	
Feminine strategies only	30%
Masculine strategies only	6%
Both feminine and masculine strategies	7%
No strategies	58%
Feminine only & feminine and masculine	37%
Masculine only & masculine and feminine	13%
Any closed-ended strategy	42%
Strategies Identified in Open-Ended Questions	
Feminine strategies only	12%
Masculine strategies only	9%
Both feminine and masculine strategies	4%
No strategies	75%
Feminine only & feminine and masculine	16%
Masculine only & masculine and feminine	13%
Any open-ended strategy	25%

NOTE: Percentages do not sum to 100 due to rounding.

crete parts. That is, most of the strategies are not unique in their character and, alone, do not sufficiently inform our understanding of the mechanisms used to manage gender.

Of those respondents who said that they employed strategies to be perceived as feminine, at least one-third chose each of the following strategies: wearing makeup off duty (31 percent), wearing makeup on duty (38 percent), wearing cologne or perfume (34 percent), wearing long hair [out of uniform] (37 percent), and wearing earrings while in uniform when permitted (37 percent).[1] Slightly fewer than one-third indicated that they wore pumps instead of flat shoes (low quarters) with the dress uniform (32 percent) and that they wore skirt uniforms instead of pants uniforms (28 percent) as strategies to be perceived as feminine. The fact that these items focus on clothing is primarily a function of the choices that were provided in the list.

It is easy to see why these strategies might be the most popular. Although they may also carry with them certain penalties, in civilian society none of these behaviors would be considered unacceptable or abnormal. While wearing high-heeled shoes, and thus being perceived as feminine, may result in a penalty, high-heeled shoes themselves are not devalued or frowned upon as might be the case with, for example, swearing. As we will see later, some of the strategies used to highlight masculinity are often negatively sanctioned in both women and men and, therefore, might not be chosen as readily as others.

Content analysis of the open-ended items revealed a wide array of strategies, some of which appeared far more often than did others. As was revealed in the closed-ended item, clothing is a key mechanism for strategizing around femininity. One woman responded that she "dressed feminine at all unit off-duty functions," while another said that she attended "functions in civilian clothing, almost always in skirts/dresses." One woman mentioned color as an important aspect in clothing choice: "I always dressed in cheerful, bright colors; but always conservatively."

One of the most interesting aspects of clothing as a strategy for being perceived as feminine was the *way* in which clothing was often worn. This is of interest not only because it goes beyond the issue of clothing *choice* but because the way in which an item was worn was often in violation of the regulations. Consider the following examples of strategies that women described: "My uniform skirt was always too short," "[I] did not wear a t-shirt under fatigues," and "I wore my BDU [battle-dress uniform] cap and Class A cap way back on my head to look more like a female." Such violations could lead to formal punishment, such as a counseling statement, or to informal punishment, such as being the subject of negative comments. In my military experience, I observed that women were frequently ridiculed for not wearing their uniforms properly. Such women were viewed as not being serious soldiers and as being more concerned about their appearance than about doing their job. Thus, though women may highlight femininity as a means of being viewed more favorably, such a strategy may have negative repercussions as well.

Women not only strategized with props such as clothing, jewelry, and makeup but also used their bodies to highlight femininity. One example of this is seen in the closed-ended item regarding hair length. As indicated earlier, 37 percent of those who said that they strategized reported that they wore their hair long as a strategy for being perceived as feminine. In the open-ended question, others referred to hair styling in general: "I tried to keep my hair in a feminine style that suited me. This involved getting a perm every 3–4 months." Another example is watching one's weight ("I kept a close watch on my weight because I was under the false assumption that 'thinness' and feminine were related").

Another strategy was the intentional avoidance of swearing. One woman wrote that she "never used bad language like many other women in [the] military do," while another wrote that she simply, "did not swear much." This issue will be of particular interest when we turn to the strategies for highlighting masculinity. Yet another strategy that appeared frequently included home and office decor ("Flowers on my desk, my Noritake coffee cup and picture frames on my desk"). In sum, consciously manipulating one's appearance and engaging in behaviors traditionally marked as "female" were common strategies for managing the perceptions others had about one's status as feminine.

All of the strategies discussed thus far focus on appearance, personal space, and personal habits. None of these strategies are particularly surprising, nor can most immediately be labeled as detrimental to one's physical or emotional well-being. The same cannot be said of the last group of strategies.

It is evident from the data that both women and men have significant roles not only in shaping ideas of femininity but in meting out the penalties for gender violations. However, the strategies discussed thus far are accomplished on an individual basis. That is, the women chose what to wear, how to wear it, and so on. In the last group of strategies, men play a key role. These strategies are those in which women intentionally engaged in social or sexual relations with men.

The closed-ended question revealed that about one woman in ten employed "social strategies", such as socializing with the men in their units (8 percent), dating men in their units (11 percent), or marrying while on active duty (8 percent) as a conscious attempt to be perceived as feminine. Five percent indicated that, as a strategy for being perceived as feminine, when they had a boyfriend, they "made sure people knew it." These numbers may seem inconsequential until we realize that this means that women are intentionally engaging in personal relationships as strategies for altering or enhancing the perceptions that others have of them. When we examine this theme as it is represented in the open-ended items, it is even more startling.

One woman wrote, "I believe I did a little 'indiscriminate' dating, more than I should have, maybe to feel more feminine." Another "made up stories re: boyfriends, het[erosexual] sex, dates; even slept with man/men (when I was drunk) to cover for myself and the company." One woman said that she "tried to date civilian men," while another said, "I felt that I *had* to have a boyfriend." A key element to understanding why such social and sexual relations with men would serve as strategies is the relationship between femininity and heterosexuality. As one woman said, "I mostly made conscious attempts to appear heterosexual v. feminine." Another woman answered, "Hanging around with nothing but males and having sex with them to prove I wasn't a lesbian." Because of its obvious link to displays of heterosexuality, it is worth noting at this point that there was an entirely separate question, not analyzed here, about strategies to avoid being perceived as lesbian. The responses provided here were given in response to the question about being perceived as feminine. This is powerful evidence of the link between the ways gender and sexuality have been constructed.

Some women took the opposite approach, downplaying sexuality to be perceived as more feminine. One respondent indicated her strategy for being perceived as feminine by simply stating, "Good, Catholic, Virginal girl." And, unlike the woman who "dressed to attract attention," another woman wrote, "I didn't want any more attention drawn to me. I received enough at work." This combination of seemingly opposite strategies parallels the way in which "woman" has often been dichotomously constructed as whore/Madonna.

A third type of question that addressed strategies was also included in the survey. Respondents were asked, "Are there other things that you did to make yourself *feel* more feminine/masculine of which others were unaware?" These strategies would not necessarily be aimed at altering the perceptions of those around the woman, though they may have that effect. This question is somewhat difficult to analyze because I realized while examining the results that the question could have been interpreted in a variety of ways. I had intended the item to refer to those behaviors to which others might be exposed (e.g., language) but that the others might not realize were linked to perceptions of gender. It became clear from the data that most respondents keyed on the issue of "feeling" and interpreted this question to mean behaviors of which others might be completely unaware (e.g., wearing silk underwear). Given these methodological difficulties, this item is best examined as a reflection of additional strategies that did not emerge in the other questions, and not as a reflection of some more narrow form of strategy.

In addition to clothing and the manner in which clothing was worn, many women often chose clothing that would be seen by few others as a means of feeling more feminine. Almost half of the women who answered the third type of question indicated that they wore "sexy" lingerie as a mechanism for feeling more feminine. This type of strategy also appeared in the open-ended question of other strategies. One woman wrote, "I wore sexy lingerie to feel better; i.e., red bras, purple panties, etc." Another respondent wrote, "When in BDUs [battle-dress uniform] I often wore teddies and sexy lingerie," while yet another said, "Wearing lacy bras or underwear underneath BDUs!" Other examples of behaviors in which women engaged to feel more feminine included indulging in bubble baths ("Hot bubble baths, facials—'girl stuff'") and, as indicated in the previous open-ended question, wearing long hair.

It was, however, not only the hair on their head that was of concern. A number of women mentioned shaving as a strategy. One woman wrote, "I kept my hair long and I shaved." Another wrote, "I was stationed in Hawaii three and a half years. . . . I shaved legs, armpits, pubic hair. I wore a bikini to the beach and loved wearing my white Sasson jeans." One woman also mentioned plucking her eyebrows as a strategy for being perceived as feminine.

In sum, the strategies aimed at increasing perceptions of femininity vary widely. The majority of those described here fit traditional markers of femininity: clothing, hair style, jewelry, and, perhaps most important, women's perceived relation to men. In some cases, two strategies that seem diametrically opposed are both used as a means toward the same end, for example, emphasizing heterosexual availability and emphasizing sexual purity. Further, behaviors that are identified as strategies are sometimes the very same behaviors that result in penalties. For example, dating many men may increase one's "femininity quotient" but may also increase the likelihood that one will be penalized for being "too feminine," for being "too" sexually available. Such a situation reinforces the belief expressed by many women that they are "damned if they do, damned if they don't." While we have seen that, regardless of these contradictions, most women who *do* strategize do so toward femininity, it is also of interest to examine those strategies employed by women who wish to be perceived as masculine.

Of those women who indicated that they employed any type of strategy, about one in eight (13 percent) indicated that they used one or more strategies aimed at highlighting masculinity. As with femininity, respondents were given a list of twenty-eight behaviors (See Methodological Appendix, survey items 122–149) and were asked to "check any of the following that you believe applied to yourself" (while on active duty). Items consisted of behaviors such as rarely wearing makeup on duty, keeping one's hair trimmed above the collar, and preferring pants uniforms to skirt uniforms. Respondents were then asked, "Do you believe that any of those behaviors checked in items 122 to 149 were part of a conscious attempt to insure that others perceived you as masculine?" Again, respondents were also asked the questions "Are there other things that you did that you believe were a conscious attempt to insure that others perceived you as masculine?" and "Are there other things that you did to make yourself feel more masculine but of which others were unaware?" As with femininity, the answers to these questions were analyzed to determine whether or not women employed strategies to be perceived as masculine and, if so, what those strategies might be.

Of the strategies listed in the survey, two were clear standouts. Three-quarters (75 percent) of the respondents who indicated employing at least one masculine strategy chose wanting to be considered "one of the guys" as a strategy. Close to half (42 percent), said that they "socialized with men" in their units as a strategy. Almost a third rarely wore makeup on duty (29 percent) or wore pants uniforms rather than skirt uniforms (28 percent) as strategies. One quarter indicated that their preferences for work uniforms (e.g., camouflage uniforms) to dress uniforms (25 percent) or casual clothing when out of uniform (25 percent) were strategies for being perceived as more masculine. Thus, clothing was also a strategy for being perceived as masculine, but not nearly as frequently as it was a strategy for being perceived as feminine. Furthermore, approximately one-quarter of the women participated in "male" sports (24 percent) and/or kept their hair trimmed above the collar (24 percent) as strategies to be seen as more masculine. When comparing the percentages, it is clear that socializing with men and being seen as "one of the guys" were dominant strategies for women who wished to be perceived as masculine.

Analysis of the open-ended items revealed strategies similar to those discussed earlier. I discovered that, with masculinity, there was little discernible difference between the two open-ended questions (i.e., the open-ended question about strategies in general and the open-ended question about strategies of which others were unaware). That is, both items contained basically the same answers. Given that, I address them together. The four main strategies that emerged are: swearing, drinking, working out, and doing other "guy things."

In the findings concerning feminine strategies, we saw that avoidance of swearing was considered by some to be a strategy for being perceived as feminine. In the results presented here, we see the opposite approach. In answer to the open-ended question about strategies, one woman wrote, "My favorite cuss word is 'shit.' I cussed when I wanted to make a point." Other examples include: "Started cursing," "Swearing," "Perhaps a bit cruder, earthier way of talking," "Talk nasty like guys, swear and stuff," "Use foul language to the extent men did," and, "Used profanity when around men." Clearly, the expression "the mouth of a sailor" held some meaning for these women, for a number of them put the cliché to work.

A number of women indicated that drinking also served as a strategy. One woman said that she drank more than she should have. Another said, "Drinking with the guys—trying to keep up." One woman, however, did not acknowledge employing strategies but then wrote, "Maybe—I tried beer because all of the guys were drinking it." Yet another mentioned "the amount of substance abuse" as a strategy for being perceived as masculine. As one woman wrote, "Foul language, smoking, drinking, joking—I am undeniably feminine—but I tried in many ways to 'compensate' (unfortunately)." While not all would agree, many people would argue that swearing and drinking are more acceptable in men than in women, especially in the military. In fact, although in the not too distant past, swearing was not viewed as inappropriate or unprofessional and drinking was not only tolerated but encouraged; however, new policies on sexual harassment and alcohol abuse have led to changes in recent years. Thus, it is not surprising that if women wished to strategize toward masculinity, they would seize on these "available" behaviors as strategies for doing so.

A third strategy described by respondents was "working out" or concentrating on physical fitness. In the military, especially in recent years, we would expect this to be a "positive" strategy because of the military's emphasis on physical fitness. In addition, if women, especially feminine women, are perceived as weak and penalized for it, then it makes sense that some women might try to insure that they are perceived as physically fit. As one woman described it, "I made sure that I was physically fit to avoid being perceived as a weak female." Another wrote, "[I] thought many other women were weak and pathetic. Made sure I was *very strong* physically." Several specifically mentioned training in weight lifting, a particularly stereotypically masculine mode of working out.

In a related vein, a number of women mentioned not allowing coworkers to help them with physical tasks. Typical responses included: "Not asking assistance of others when lifting heavy things" and "[I] lifted heavier things on the job than I should have." Another wrote:

> I did not let others (men) help me, unless a job normally required 2 people, and the guy was *assigned* to work with me. I only asked other women to help me, or went to great lengths to use leverage and improvise. (Enlisted, Navy, heterosexual)

Demonstration of physical strength, whether through physical development or task accomplishment, is apparently one mechanism by which women try to be perceived as masculine and, therefore, as fitting in.

Though the last decade has led to significant change in this arena, the strategy of "working out," especially weight lifting, is viewed by some as "doing guy things." Some would say the same of swearing and drinking. If this weren't the case, then it is unlikely that these would be identified as strategies for being perceived as masculine. Yet, the frequency with which these behaviors were mentioned warranted their being considered separate categories. The fourth strategy, "doing guy things," stands separate from these behaviors.

Women mentioned a variety of behaviors, apart from the three already discussed, that they exhibited as a means of being perceived as masculine. In some cases, these were specific behaviors ("Learned to scuba and skydive"); in others, they were general statements ("Go out with the guys and do the types of things they like to do"). The following comments illustrate these findings: "I drove a Pinto station wagon with a tool box in the back. I did my own oil changes," "Talked about stuff I did as a civilian—played in rock band, rode motorcycle, etc.," "Auto hobby shop—fixed guys' cars—took flying lessons and mechanics with the guys." Again, certain behaviors and hobbies are culturally defined as masculine. If participation in these events is readily available, then it is understandable that they would enter the repertoire of some women who wish to be perceived as masculine.

Another area of the strategy of "doing guy things" is what we might consider demeanor. One woman discussed "using the language and mannerisms of men," while another said she "became more assertive/aggressive." One woman said she "learned to be aggressive when necessary," while another said, "High assertiveness; low exhibited emotionality." As one woman described it, "[I] developed a tougher attitude and tried to hide my softer side at work." In some cases the adoption of male demeanor was more generalized. One woman said that she "emulated military men's attitudes and reflected their opinions," while another wrote, "I made sure I was as 'gung-ho' as the guys on my flights and earned a rep as being as tough or tougher than any of them."

Akin to the strategy of "doing guy things" was the strategy of *not* doing "female things." One woman "attempted to downplay feminine 'traits' such as gossiping, flowers on desk, being emotional." Yet another wrote:

> Whenever I deployed, I reduced my attachment to "feminine" stuff; no contacts, no makeup, no complaints if I couldn't shower/wash hair, no perfume—made fun of women who continued these trappings while deployed. (Lieutenant, Navy, heterosexual)[2]

In some instances, and as would be the case with some weight lifters, such behaviors involved physical change. One woman said, "I didn't wear makeup, I never swayed my hips, I strode along." Another said, "I kept my fingernails short and never polished them!" To some degree, the absence of the feminine may be seen, by default, as an approximation of the masculine. This is similar to Nancy Chodorow's (1978) claim that boys, and men, define what is masculine by virtue of its *not* being feminine.

My results show that the types of strategies employed by women seeking to manage gender are numerous and diverse. Whether one is trying to be perceived as feminine or masculine, there is an available repertoire of strategies that one may choose to employ. As I have shown, close to half of the women in this sample acknowledge the employment of strategies to manage gender. While most opt toward femininity, some do strategize toward masculinity. Can we predict who is more likely to engage in one type of strategy or the other?

Who Uses Strategies?

In my discussion of pressures and penalties, I showed that they were sometimes significantly related to various characteristics such as branch, rank, and sexual orientation. In the case of both feminine and masculine strategies, I found significant relationships only between measures of strategizing and whether one's rank is junior or senior. Of those respondents who indicated that they engaged in at least one closed-ended strategy, whether feminine or masculine, about two-thirds (65 percent) were junior and one-third (35 percent) senior, while those who did not do so were split almost evenly, with about half (48 percent) being junior and half (52 percent) being senior. Of all junior personnel, half indicated that they did employ these strategies, while half did not. For senior personnel, two-thirds (67 percent) indicated that they did not engage in strategies, while one-third (33 percent) did so.

When examining only the measure for strategizing around femininity, the relationship with rank remained strong. Almost one-third (29 percent) of senior personnel indicated that they engaged in such strategies. In comparison, 43 percent of junior personnel said that they engaged in strategies toward femininity. Of the more than one-third of the sample (37 percent) who engaged in strategies of femininity, almost two-thirds (65 percent) were junior personnel.

When examining the measure for strategizing around masculinity, the relationship with rank was also strong. Six percent of senior personnel indicated that they engaged in such strategies, while close to one in five (18 percent) of junior personnel did so. Though only about one in eight (13 percent) of all respondents engaged in strategies of masculinity, of those who did, more than three-quarters (78 percent) were junior personnel. Thus, one's status as junior or senior is significantly related to whether one uses strategies for managing gender, with junior personnel more likely to engage in either type of strategy. It is, however, of interest to note that senior personnel are about five times more likely to engage in strategies of femininity than of masculinity, whereas junior personnel are only about two and half times more likely to engage in strategies of femininity compared to masculinity.

The relationship between strategizing around masculinity and sexual orientation was also significant. One in five (19 percent) of the lesbian and bisexual women indicated that they engaged in strategies of masculinity, while only one in ten (10 percent) of heterosexual women did so.

Compared to a woman who does not describe herself as feminine, a woman who does describe herself as feminine is about three times as likely to engage in feminine strategies. Women who describe themselves as masculine, compared to those who do not, are more than four times as likely to engage in masculine strategies. Why might this be the case? What is the relationship between self-perceptions of gender and the strategies that one employs? Though these data cannot provide the answer, it is worth speculating on the issue.

Did women select strategies on the basis of their self-perception as feminine or masculine? Or, did women come to see themselves as feminine or masculine as a result of the employment of gendered strategies? It is possible that both processes operate simultaneously. I argue that we select strategies from what we perceive to be an available repertoire. In addition, strategies may be marked as available or unavailable, depending upon how we perceive ourselves. For example, a woman who perceives herself as feminine, for social and cultural reasons, may view weight lifting as an "unavailable" strategy. Wearing earrings or skirts would, however, be marked as an "available strategy." On the other hand, a woman who perceives herself as masculine may view wearing skirts as an "unavailable" strategy, while weight lifting is marked as "available." Such definitions are clearly a result of social and cultural prescriptions of the feminine and the masculine. Women may select strategies to be consistent with existing self-perceptions.

I also argue that it is not the "unavailable" strategies on which we should focus our attention but the "available" strategies. Those marked, whether by default or otherwise, as "unavailable" simply do not enter the repertoire. It is those strategies that are "available" that enter the repertoire, may be selected by the individual for use as a strategy, and, therefore, reinforce the self-perception that already exists. Thus, women who see themselves as feminine choose feminine strategies, and women who see themselves as masculine choose masculine strategies. These choices then reinforce gendered self-perceptions.

Such a dynamic illustrates that the acquisition and display of gender is the result not only of early socialization and internalization but of the continual reinforcement of gender. That is, our "gender repertoire" may be acquired over time as a result of socialization and internalization around gender. But, the use of that repertoire throughout our lives serves to continually create and re-create what gender—femininity or masculinity—means and where we see ourselves as fitting into social and cultural notions of femininity and masculinity. We become our own "victims," limited in our gender display because of the limited repertoire that we feel is available to us for the expression of our gendered selves. This scenario suggests that it is quite possible and, I argue, likely that, as a result of choosing gendered strategies, individuals reinforce existing self-perceptions of gender type.

Does self-perception lead to the employment of certain strategies, or vice versa? I argue that both are possible but that it is likely that we come to a setting—in this case, the military—with a particular self-perception and repertoire, both gendered, and that the choices we make reinforce both our self-perceptions as well as our available repertoires. The importance of this discussion to the work presented here is twofold. First, we must consider the direction of the effect that we observe in the model; second, and most important, this dynamic illustrates the conceptualization of gender as something that we *do*, rather than simply something that we may *be*.

Are there other predictors for the strategies in which we engage? Analyses of these results suggest not. Even the significant relationships between strategies and rank, as measured by junior/senior status, and masculine strategies and sexual orientation fail to hold when controls are introduced. Rather than view this as an absence of findings, I believe that it suggests that there is little discernible difference, on the variables considered, between those who do or do not strategize toward femininity and between those who do and do not strategize toward masculinity. Does this mean that there are *no* differences? Probably not. There may well be measures not available in these data that would hold some predictive power. For example, *which people* come to see themselves as feminine or masculine, and why? It is quite likely that there are social psychological influences not addressed by these data. In sum, while these findings do not support the existence of other characteristics that predict strategy selection I cannot claim that such characteristics do not exist.

A Framework for Strategizing

"Strategies," as they have been defined in this research, have consisted of two basic types: feminine strategies and mascu-

TABLE 4.2
Distribution of Closed-Ended Strategies,
Sub-sample[3]

Feminine strategies only	70%
Feminine and masculine strategies	17%
Masculine strategies only	13%

line strategies. Women may engage in only one or in both types of strategies.

Table 4.2 shows that, of those women who indicated employing any closed-ended strategy, close to three-quarters employed strategies toward femininity only. About one in eight employed strategies toward masculinity only, while about one in six employed both feminine and masculine strategies. Thus, of those women who do acknowledge strategizing to manage gender, most strategize toward femininity.

As discussed earlier, I believed that some women would strategize toward femininity and some toward masculinity and that some would employ both types of strategies. In designing this research, I imagined that women would employ one of these three strategies as a mechanism for the management of gender perceptions. After all, gender is salient not only throughout society but particularly in settings where women are a minority. That framework led me to focus my question design on actions to accentuate femininity or masculinity, or both. The final instrument was not adequately designed to deal with a fourth possibility, the *minimizing* of femininity and/or masculinity. I suggest that there exists an alternative framework for the conceptualization of gender strategizing, a framework in which there are four possibilities for the management of gender: femininity, masculinity, balanced, and neuter.

Why might three out of four women who employ strategies to manage gender choose to emphasize femininity only? In the course of designing this research, I chose not to pose formal hypotheses. Had I done so, in fact, I would have speculated that most women, if they recognized strategizing at all, would strategize toward masculinity. Given the devaluation of the feminine, both across society and especially within the context of the military, I would have imagined that women would emphasized masculinity as a way of "fitting in." I would have been wrong. Why might women choose to highlight femininity over masculinity or over a blending of both gender types?

As discussed earlier, individuals acquire a repertoire of available gender skills, or strategies, as they are socialized as members of society and as members of a given group, in this case the military. In this sample, a majority of women (75 percent) indicated that they would describe themselves as feminine. If women possess a repertoire that is consistent with how they perceive themselves, and if women employ strategies from that repertoire, then the fact that most women are socialized toward femininity suggests that more women have a "feminine repertoire" of available strategies than have a "masculine repertoire." Simply put, one's repertoire is defined by the social and cultural milieu in which one operates. Thus, we would expect to see more women utilizing feminine strategies of gender management than we would masculine.

This argument considers social action without taking into account the specific context. What happens when the context in which one is strategizing provides contradictory information about the value of certain gendered behaviors? Women do believe there are penalties for being perceived as "too feminine." Why, under these conditions, would women continue to strategize toward femininity?

As I have indicated, we can use only those tools available to us. The strategies that most women have at their disposal, or feel that they have at their disposal, are primarily feminine. Props such as earrings, perfume, and makeup are not only available but easy to employ. In addition, there are simply many more "feminine props" than there are masculine, for women or men. Women have a much greater selection of jewelry, cosmetics, and other accoutrements than do men. Conversely, most women have a more limited "masculine repertoire" available to them. As a result of socialization and opportunity, women have fewer masculine strategies from which to choose. Also, many of the strategies that would heighten masculinity have negative connotations, perhaps even more so for women. For example, swearing and drinking may heighten perceptions of masculinity, but have other repercussions as well. Thus, women may opt for femininity by default as much as socialization. I will return to this issue when I address masculine strategies.

There appears to be little doubt that while both femininity in women and masculinity in women may result in penalties, the penalties for masculinity may be far greater. Recall that close to two-thirds of the women who believed that there are penalties for being perceived as too masculine listed being perceived as a lesbian as the main penalty. A military woman who is seen as a lesbian, regardless of how she identifies herself, faces not only the informal homophobia that the military has in common with the rest of society but also faces the threat of being forced out of the military. As one woman wrote, "Why would I want to appear masculine? Women in the military have to combat being labeled as 'dykes'—masculine behavior is not what they seek." In essence, it is probably better to be perceived as an "incompetent, heterosexual slut" than a lesbian, competent or not.

If these arguments hold true, why do some women choose masculine strategies? Some women may have acquired, or may prefer to acquire, a masculine repertoire. In these cases, this may be the more comfortable strategy to pursue. For those women who, for example, prefer mechanics over mascara, this may be the favored approach. In short, while the majority of women may have acquired a feminine repertoire, we cannot expected this to be true for all women.

It appears that, for some women, being perceived as feminine is viewed as so problematic that to be perceived as masculine is the only alternative. Another possibility is that women in the military are generally in the position of having to learn from other men. In discussing her leadership style, one woman wrote, "I had no female role models to know that there was an alternative women-styled leadership role." Others would argue that even when such a role is available, it is less rewarded and more likely to be penalized when compared to "male-style" leadership. The military, like many professional settings, views "male" leadership style as the "right" leadership style. One woman said, "Most men in the military perceive leadership as a masculine quality." As another wrote, "If a woman doesn't adopt male mannerisms, she is 'too feminine' to be a leader." Thus, some women believe that being perceived as masculine is the best strategy for success in the male world of the military.

As shown in Table 4.2, of those women who strategized at all, about one in six indicated that she engaged in both feminine and masculine strategies. I believe this combination approach is comparable to the "blending" strategy described by Sheppard (1989). By drawing on a mixed repertoire, women are seeking to be feminine enough to be accepted as women, heterosexual women at that, yet masculine enough to be accepted as soldiers.

By employing a variety of strategies, both feminine and masculine, women may increase the odds of avoiding penalties. Yet, it is reasonable to wonder whether employing both types of strategies could lead to penalties rather than acceptance. After all, if one is perceived as "too feminine" or "too masculine," penalties are likely to occur. I believe that it is the modifier "too" that is critical in this situation. By utilizing both types of strategies, women avoid being seen as "too" anything. A delicate balance between the feminine and the masculine is struck in which each tempers the other. One respondent indicated:

> I feel more masculine but felt that either extreme of femininity or masculinity was persecuted by male counterparts. I had to strike a balance in other's perceptions of me. I couldn't be myself. (Enlisted, Army, bisexual)

The theme of "balance" between feminine and masculine appeared in a number of responses. As one woman wrote, "I believe that there is a very delicate balance that the vast majority of women cannot achieve in the waging debate of 'masculine' vs. 'feminine.'" Another woman noted, "We cannot always be just 'feminine' or 'masculine.' I found myself being a combination of both at times, it all depends on who you're dealing with."

Thus, for some women, heightening femininity alone or masculinity alone is not the preferred strategy. Some women seek to exhibit both and, presumably, to gain the positive effects of both or, at the very least, to allow the negative effects of each to cancel each other out. But, what about those who offered information that did not fit within the structure provided in the survey design, that is, those who suggested that the *lack* of gender was their strategy?

The fourth category within the framework for strategizing is what I term "neuter," a description provided by some respondents. One wrote:

> I used to joke about being Air Force neuter. It never felt like I was feminine or masculine—never enough of the qualities of either to fit in a category easily. I always attempted to play down sexuality. (Captain, Air Force, heterosexual)

It is important to clarify the distinction I make between balanced, meaning a combination of feminine and masculine, and neuter. By neuter I refer to attempts to render notions of either feminine and masculine absent from one's presentation of self.

Roughly speaking, for every ten women who acknowledge the employment of strategies to manage gender (i.e., femininity, masculinity, or both), about seven choose femininity, two choose balance, and one chooses masculinity. But, about six out of every ten women in the sample did not acknowledge employing any of these strategies. While some of these women indicated in open-ended items that they strategized toward the absence of gender, it is important to note that strategizing to be seen as "neutral" is not the same as claiming not to strategize at all. Some women believed that they were able to just "be themselves." There is virtually no way of ascertaining how accurate their recollections may be. I believe, again, that we can conclude that the indications of strategizing reflected in these data are a conservative account of who engages in conscious strategizing around gender.

As discussed earlier, the original research design did not account for the possibility that some women might not wish to heighten either femininity or masculinity. Though I had failed to design measures for the minimizing of gender I was fortunate in that this strategy was revealed to me in the open-ended items.

The strategy of being neuter is, perhaps, the most disturbing. In trying to downplay any sense of gender or sexuality, women are, in some fashion, seeking to neutralize a presumably important part of who they are. In essence, they don't want to be seen as what they are; yet they don't wish to be seen as that which they are not. Why would anyone seek to employ such a strategy? Women seek to deny their gender and deny their sexuality, for it is far more difficult to penalize that which is absent. One respondent indicated, "For the first ten years I tried to be a-sexual." As individuals, it is easier to target behaviors, props, and so on. It is, without question, more difficult to attack that which we cannot see.

Summary

Although many specific strategies were revealed in this study, the following table illustrates the typology for strategizing around gender that emerged:

TABLE 4.3
A Typology for Strategizing Around Gender

Femininity	Employ feminine strategies only
Masculinity	Employ masculine strategies only
Balanced	Employ both feminine and masculine strategies
Neuter	Minimize both feminine and masculine cues

Close to half of the women in this sample employ some form of strategy for the management of gender. Of those who do, most elect to employ strategies of femininity. I argue that one reason that this may be the case is that, as social actors, we acquire a repertoire of strategies for gender management, a repertoire that is often closely linked to how we, and others, see ourselves as gendered beings. A second reason is that the link between gender and sexuality leaves women with little choice.

The ability of society to penalize "gender-deviant" behaviors requires the presence of two conditions. First, behaviors must be defined as gendered so that behaviors are viewed as being predominantly "female" or "male" and that, when they are observed in individuals of the sex for which they are deemed inappropriate, they are interpreted as deviant. Even today, most people would have little trouble, whether they agreed personally or not, with providing "society's gender label" for a variety of behaviors. Thus, the first condition is met by virtue of the perpetuation of beliefs that some things are "feminine" and some things are "masculine." I am not making the case that *all* behaviors are so identified. I do, however, insist that even today the vast majority of the populace would have little trouble labeling personal characteristics (e.g., strong, emotional, assertive, caring) as "feminine" or "masculine."

Second, penalties must exist that are separate from, yet undeniably linked with, gender. In contemporary Western society, though not in those societies only, these penalties are situated in our attitudes toward and beliefs about sexuality. There are two key aspects to this relationship. The first is that ideas about sexual activity in general are gendered. Historically, women have been viewed as lustful, men as rational. While this specific view may no longer be central to philosophical and social theory, other gendered aspects of sexuality persist. Even in contemporary society, many believe that women's sexuality is to *be* controlled, while men's sexuality *exerts* control. The second key aspect is that gender-deviant behavior is an indication of homosexuality and, conversely, that homosexuality suggests gender deviance.

Thus, gender deviance is subject to penalty not only by virtue of the definition of certain behaviors as deviant but because we have at our disposal a deeply entrenched mechanism for censuring any such deviance. That mechanism is the relationship between gender and sexuality.

DOING GENDER / DOING SEXUALITY

> One of the hardest parts of being a military woman is just the constant scrutiny and criticism. Act "too masculine" and you're accused of being a dyke; act "too feminine" and you're either accused of sleeping around, or you're not serious; you're just there to get a man.
>
> —Lieutenant, Navy, bisexual

As the quotation suggests, women in the military live under a microscope. They are faced with daily challenges about their right to be in the military, their ability to do the job, and, often, their sexuality. As social actors in a world where gender is very important, we all routinely engage in behaviors that are gendered; we also *do* gender. Women in the military must do gender in such a way as to carefully negotiate terrain that often appears designed to make the venture as difficult as possible. While I have provided evidence of the impact of these dynamics on the lives of military women, I now turn to the broader question of what we can learn by examining gender as active rather than static, as something we do rather than as what we are. West and Zimmerman (1987) ask three questions that provide an excellent framework for answering that question:

> If, for example, individuals strive to achieve gender in encounters with others, how does a culture instill the need to achieve it? What is the relationship between the production of gender at the level of interaction and such institutional arrangements as the division of labor in society? And, perhaps most important, how does doing gender contribute to the subordination of women by men? (140)

This book is an attempt to determine what types of strategies women employ, if any, to manage others' perceptions of them regarding the degree to which they are perceived as feminine or masculine. I have utilized the theoretical perspective of "doing gender" to frame this inquiry. A reasonable question that might be raised is whether or not the evidence provided here, in fact, constitutes "doing gender."

In "Doing Gender," West and Zimmerman write, "Gender depictions are less a consequence of our 'essential sexual natures' than interactional portrayals of what we would like to convey about sexual natures, using conventionalized gestures" (1987: 130). The idea that we engage in various actions to manage what we "would like to convey" is central to the research presented here. The strategies discussed in this book are those strategies in which women engage specifically to manage how they are perceived by those around them. More recently, West and Fenstermaker (1995) have written:

> . . . the notion of accountability is relevant not only to activities that conform to prevailing normative conceptions (i.e., activities that are conducted "unremarkably," and thus, do not warrant more than a passing glance) but also to those activities that deviate. The issue is not deviance or conformity; rather it is the possible evaluation of action in relation to normative conceptions and the likely consequence of that evaluation for subsequent interaction. (21)

Thus, though the concept of "doing gender" also refers to broader cognitive processes, it seems clear that West and Zimmerman, and more recently Fenstermaker, also intend for the concept to include actions in which we consciously engage as a means by which to "manipulate" the potential consequences of our interactions. When women in the military consciously choose to dress a particular way, for example, or to play (or not play) a particular sport, they are doing gender. They are aware of how their actions will be evaluated, "relative to normative conceptions," and understand the "consequence of that evaluation for subsequent interaction." As shown by the data, the consequences include a wide range of penalties that most women wish to avoid.

One might pose the question of whether or not this begs a more rational choice framework than one of interactional work. I do not believe them to be mutually exclusive. Understanding that a given action may lead to an undesirable result and acting to avoid the undesirable result may be understood as a rational act. It does not, however, preclude the action from being interactional in nature.

Furthermore, in this research I have shown that, in many cases, either "choice" (i.e., to strategize toward femininity or to strategize toward masculinity) may contradict assumptions of rationality. That is, engaging in one presumably "rational act" (e.g., wearing a skirt to avoid suspicions of lesbianism) may also lack "rationality" because by heightening the feminine, other penalties (e.g., the label of slut) may be incurred. Likewise, to engage in "masculine" behaviors to insure that one is perceived as a "good soldier" may have its own penalty (e.g., the label of lesbian). Thus, while a rational choice model may be appropriate in that the women engage in various strategies to avoid penalties, the reality is that those strategies are just as likely to result in penalties, albeit of a different nature. An examination of the choices women make and *how* both actions and consequences are structured by interaction is far better served by a theoretical framework in which interaction itself is the dominant theme.

By consciously engaging in behaviors intended to manipulate both perception and subsequent interaction, women are doing gender. They are creating and recreating not only what it means to be a woman but what it means to be a woman in the military. The evidence presented here strongly supports a reconceptualization of gender as something we *do*, more than something we simply possess.

The first question posed by West and Zimmerman is how a culture instills the need to achieve gender. By examining the process by which young children act to be seen as socially competent, they conclude that:

> . . . gender differences, or the sociocultural shaping of "essential female and male natures," achieve the status of objective facts. They are rendered normal, natural features

of persons and provide the tacit rationale for differing
fates of women and men within the social order. (142)

By establishing ideas about what is essentially female or male,
what is "normal" or "natural," the culture instills within us a
need to maintain these gendered identities. That is, we must
continually create and recreate our identities as gendered beings.

If we consider the demands of our culture to be part of the
process of socialization and internalization, how does "doing
gender" differ from these processes? First, to suggest that gender is a process does not mean that we do not also acquire notions of femininity and masculinity through mechanisms of
socialization and internalization. I see the process of doing
gender as an extension of theories of socialization and internalization.

Through socialization and internalization, we learn the
"gender rules." But, who we are as gendered beings is not cast
in stone at a particular age. Just as socialization in general is
a lifelong process, so, too, is the process by which we create
and re-create gender and who we are as gendered beings. We
might think of socialization and internalization as the process
by which we learn the rules and go on automatic pilot, acting
in some instances with little conscious thought to our gendered interactions with others. But, as this research illustrates,
there are situations in which we are very conscious of how we
deploy gender, how we manipulate how others perceive us in
terms of femininity and masculinity. Whether a woman, without thinking, steps aside to allow a male to open the door for
her or whether she intentionally does so is not the issue. The

fact is that in each scenario, gender is used in the interaction to convey something about who we are and the relationship of one actor to the other.

My focus thus far has been gender. But, there is another important mechanism for insuring that we feel compelled to engage in the active accomplishment of gender—sexuality. As discussed earlier, there are at least two ways in which sexuality functions to reinforce our need to do gender. First, notions of what types of sexual behavior are appropriate are used to insure that women work to be seen as "good women." For example, a woman who does not want to be viewed as a "whore" or a "tramp" must modify her appearance, and possibly her demeanor, so that she fits "acceptable" ideas of how a "good woman" looks or acts. Similarly, men who have a certain "look" are assumed to possess, or not possess, a degree of sexual prowess.

Second, perceptions of gender are used to make assessments of one's sexual orientation. In women, femininity implies heterosexuality, while masculinity implies homosexuality. This may work in the opposite fashion, as well. A woman known to be a lesbian may be assumed to possess more masculine traits than her heterosexual counterpart. Thus, perceptions about one are used to make inferences about the other.

It is critical, however, to understand that the relationship between gender and sexuality can function in this way only in the presence of other factors. These factors are the broader social and cultural beliefs about sexuality and gender. First, there must exist ideas about sexuality as being composed of the good versus the bad. If all sexuality, including homosexuality, were viewed positively, there would be no negative labels (e.g., whore or tramp) available to us. If there were nothing "wrong" with being labeled a lesbian, the threat of the label would not exist.

Second, there must exist ideas about gender, about femininity and masculinity, that allow us to view certain gendered behaviors as appropriate and inappropriate for women or men. This is achieved through the assumption that women should be feminine (or do femininity) and men should be masculine (or do masculinity). Add to the expectation of what we should *be* or *do* expectations about what we must *not be* (i.e., masculinity is *in*appropriate in women and femininity is *in*appropriate in men) and we further solidify social perceptions of which gendered behaviors are appropriate for whom.

Thus, our culture instills the need to achieve gender by threatening social actors with penalties for violating prescribed notions of acceptable gendered behavior and acceptable sexual behavior. By linking the two together, we insure that violations in either arena result in penalties. Specifically, and because gendered behaviors are the more visible, the threat of being labeled as sexually deviant may function to insure that we "do gender" in the appropriate fashion. That is, women enact femininity, and men enact masculinity.

It should be noted that West and Fenstermaker (1993) make clear that "doing gender does not always mean living up to normative conceptions of femininity or masculinity" (157). But, they also note, "To the extent that members of society know their actions are accountable, they will design their actions in relation to how they might be seen and described by others." They write:

> First, and perhaps most important, conceiving of gender as an ongoing accomplishment, accountable to interaction, implies that we must locate its emergence in *social situations*, rather than within the individual or some ill-defined set of role expectations. . . . What it involves is crafting conduct that can be evaluated in relation to normative conceptions of manly and womanly natures . . . and assessing conduct in light of those conceptions—given the situation at hand. (157)

The social situation in which femininity serves as an indicator of heterosexuality can call forth the enactment of femininity only if there is some reason to want to insure that one is perceived to be heterosexual. Sociocultural attitudes toward homosexuality function to insure that this is the case. But, in the case of the research presented here, there is an additional "social situation" in which such actions are located. That situation is the military ban on lesbians, gay men, and bisexuals.

The findings presented here highlight the fact that to be perceived as masculine may result in being labeled a lesbian. Not only may women be "shunned," or lose the respect of their peers, but the institutional prohibition against lesbians and gay men may result in investigation and, ultimately, discharge. One way of avoiding such charges is to insure that one is perceived as feminine and, thus, heterosexual. While I do not argue that this is the sole explanation for women who engage in feminine strategies, I do believe that it must be viewed as a significant factor. As a number of women indicated, it was more important to be perceived as heterosexual than as feminine.

Thus, we feel compelled to do gender not only because of the way in which we are socialized but because of the social situation in which we find ourselves. In this instance, the link between gender and sexuality *and* both societal and institutional attitudes toward homosexuality function to insure that most women choose to enact strategies aimed at highlighting their femininity, thus insuring that they are perceived as heterosexual. In short, this process instills in individuals a need to "achieve gender" in their encounters with others.

The second question posed by West and Zimmerman (1987) is: "What is the relationship between the production of gender at the level of interaction and such institutional arrangements as the division of labor in society?" In the case of the military, gender is produced at the level of interaction, but the result is the reinforcement of perceptions of women as unfit for military service. These perceptions are not merely microlevel assessments that some individuals hold but perceptions that permeate the broader institution. When the majority of women can be labeled "feminine," and anything feminine is viewed as inconsistent with military service, women, as a group, can become viewed as "inconsistent" with, or less than capable of performing, military service. Thus, producing gender at the level of interaction (e.g., enacting femininity) creates and maintains broader institutional arrangements in which women are perceived to be second-class soldiers.

Many of the women in this study indicated that they felt pressure to act more feminine or more masculine than they would have otherwise. Even more women noted that there were penalties for women who were perceived as too feminine or too masculine. Regardless of whether women are feminine or masculine, the potential penalty is discharge. If women are aggressive, they are lesbians; if women are not aggressive enough, they may be viewed as incapable of leading troops and may receive poor evaluation reviews. In either case, the ultimate penalty can be discharge. At the least, women as a group are subject to the label of "unfit." Women have to prove themselves the exception to the rule.

One interesting example that supports this position is that of the male sergeant who, together with a female flight surgeon, was captured by the Iraqis during the Persian Gulf War. After their experience as prisoners of war, he acknowledged that she could fight alongside him any day but added that he wasn't prepared to say the same for all women. Sergeant Troy Dunlap stated, "I was really amazed . . . I was overwhelmed by the way she handled herself. . . . She can go to combat with me anytime" (Dateline NBC 1992). He made it clear that she was the exception. One woman had proven herself; women as a group remained questionable. As Major Rhonda Cornum said in response, "I don't think I'll ever change his mind that says that women as a category of people shouldn't go to combat, but I think I did change his mind that this one individual person who happens to be female can go" (Dateline NBC 1992).

When women enact femininity, they are not being good soldiers. When they are "good soldiers," they risk being labeled lesbians. It is not difficult to imagine how women who fit this description, *regardless of sexual orientation*, may be labeled lesbian. Thus, the enactment of gender at the interactional level has the potential to reinforce perceptions of women as inappropriate for military service for a number of reasons. Such a perception of women then reinforces the belief that men are somehow uniquely suited to serving in the nation's military. The production of gender at the interactional level reinforces both ideological and institutional arrangements that place women at the margins of military participation.

The third question posed by West and Zimmerman (1987) is "How does doing gender contribute to the subordination of women by men?" If, as described earlier, women are perceived as second-class soldiers, or as less than capable, it is not far-fetched to argue that women are being subordinated by men. It is important to reiterate that clearly not all women, as individuals, are seen as second rate or unsuccessful. There are thousands of women who have served admirably and have won the respect of their male coworkers, peers and superiors alike. Nevertheless, I maintain that women *as a group* are viewed as second class and are subordinated by the men of the military.

Whether women are sexually harassed, denied assignments, or prohibited from performing particular jobs, we must realize that it is not simply their poor performance that allows such incidents to occur. The social and institutional arrangements that permit women to be viewed as poor substitutes for male soldiers subordinate women to men and limit their participation as full members of the military. In some cases, attributions of inadequacy have followed women to their deaths.

Lieutenant Kara Hultgreen was one of the first women to qualify to fly a naval fighter jet, the F-14. Lt. Hultgreen died on October 25, 1994, when she crashed in the Pacific during a training exercise. The rumor mill in the Navy immediately spun into action, the MINERVA Center reporting that:

> ... [some went] so far as to send out false information in anonymous phone calls and faxes purporting that Hultgreen was unqualified and received special treatment by a politically correct Navy. In fact, Hultgreen was third out of seven flyers in her class. (*Minerva's Bulletin Board*, Fall/Winter 1994: 3).

Subsequent investigation revealed that the aircraft had lost an engine and that even more skilled pilots would have had a difficult time landing successfully. Commander Trish Beckman, president of Women Military Aviators, writes:

> A combination of factors and limited time to recognize and correct them, put Kara in a "deep hole" which cost her life (and would have done the same to skilled Test Pilots in the same situation). What is different in this circumstance is that unnamed Navy men have attempted to slander and libel her reputation publicly (something that has never been done to a deceased male aviator, no matter how incompetent he was known to be or how many lives he took with him). (*Minerva's Bulletin Board* Fall/Winter 1994: 3–4)

In contrast, when two Navy pilots flew their naval helicopter over the demilitarized zone into Korea in December 1994, resulting in the death of one and the capture of the other, no mention was made of blame or incompetence. No one suggested that perhaps permitting men to fly was a mistake.

When military women enact femininity, they are subject to accusations that they are not capable of performing tasks that have been labeled as "masculine." When military women enact masculinity, they are subject to accusations that range from lesbianism to incompetence. That is, even if they are doing "men's work" (e.g., flying combat aircraft), they cannot do it as well as men. In "doing gender," women subject themselves to an endless range of accusations, which together result in the subordination of women as a class of citizens. The question then remains, Is it possible to avoid doing gender?

West and Zimmerman (1987) write:

> If we do gender appropriately, we simultaneously sustain, reproduce, and render legitimate the institutional arrangements that are based on sex category. If we fail to do gender appropriately, we as individuals—not the institutional arrangements—may be called to account (for our character, motives, and predispositions). (146)

I believe that it is unlikely that we can avoid doing gender. Many, in fact, argue that such a goal is not desirable. But, we can alter the meaning and, more important, the consequences of doing gender.

The foregoing discussion has sought to address the questions raised by West and Zimmerman (1987). In particular, I wished to illustrate how this research provides empirical evidence for the fact that 1) gender is something we do, as opposed to something we simply possess, and 2) that, given current social arrangements, "doing gender" disadvantages women, in this case, military women.

By illustrating that we make conscious choices about how to enact gender, whether toward femininity or toward masculinity, I have provided evidence that supports the contention that we actively create and re-create gender. In doing so, we also insure that broader social notions of gender are maintained. In turn, we insure the hegemony of heterosexuality.

There are some very real implications of these findings for women's day-to-day participation in the military. Women are likely to be subjected to a variety of unpleasantries, ranging from sexual harassment to shunning, from being denied access to schooling to being denied promotions. While the penalties are varied, they share one potential outcome. All of the penalties discussed in this research may cause women to be discharged or to feel compelled to leave the service. Thus, the major implication of this research is that the perpetuation of an ideology in which soldiering and masculinity are closely bound results in the perpetuation of a military that is not only ideologically male but numerically male, as well.

While, given the existing social order, it is unlikely that we can avoid doing gender, we can begin to tackle the resulting inequities in a number of ways. We must challenge the institutional and cultural arrangements that perpetuate distinctions made on the basis of sex, or sex category.

At the interactional level we must begin to work toward the elimination of unnecessary dichotomies. This is not to say that there should not exist notions of femininity and masculinity but to argue that their assumed essential natures should be discarded. The concepts of the feminine and the masculine may possess some utility, as do ideas of emotion or reason, expression or instrumentality, and so on. But, their assignment to women and men, respectively, serve no purpose. By reconceptualizing what gender means and how we react to it, we can begin to move toward a social order in which actors are assessed on the basis of their abilities, rather than on the basis of their genitals and of a culturally defined position as feminine or masculine.

There are several mechanisms that function to keep the military "male." In addition to resulting in women's leaving the service, whether by force or by choice, perceptions of the military as male also limit the numbers of women who will consider the military as a career option. While it is unclear what the effect of the recent sexual harassment cases may be, the proportion of women enlisting in the military *has* been on the rise, primarily because of a smaller pool of military-aged youth and a decreasing propensity among youth aged 16 to 21 to enlist (*Minerva's Bulletin Board*, Spring 1994: 1–2). Recruiters are turning to women to fill the void created by the decreased availability and interest of young men. Thus, it is difficult to determine if women are finding the military more attractive than they have in the past or whether the smaller number of male recruits is inflating the proportion of female recruits. The significant indicator will be whether or not, over time, we observe a corresponding increase in the proportion of women throughout the military.

In addition, the ideology of the "male military" and legal restrictions on the participation of women function together to limit the number of positions open to women. Thus, fewer women, compared to men, can enter the service; even if huge numbers of women wished to enlist, the number of actual enlistees would be suppressed by the comparatively few positions available to them. This is especially true in the Army, where a large number of jobs are designated combat arms and are, therefore, off limits to women.

As long as the military is viewed as the domain of men, women will be outsiders and their participation will be challenged, thus perpetuating a cycle of male dominance: the military is defined as male, a small proportion of women are allowed to participate, the participation of women is challenged and penalized, the military remains ideologically and numerically male dominated, the number of women remains small. How can this cycle be broken? I believe that there are several ways in which we can disrupt such a cycle. The first is to challenge cultural constructions of sex and gender. The second is to challenge institutional arrangements that allow the perpetuation of distinctions on the basis of sex.

The first of these institutional arrangements is the classification of job eligibility by sex, that is, one is eligible for certain jobs only if one is male. In the military this is true only for those jobs coded as having a high likelihood of engaging the enemy. Women, as a group, are thus excluded from some specific occupations and some specific assignments. Barriers are being broken, but many remain. As long as women are eligible for only some jobs, they will be viewed as second-class soldiers (or sailors, "airmen," and so on). If we eliminate such barriers and assign individuals on the basis of their performance and ability it is likely that we will see a corresponding increase in the acceptance of women as participants in the military. I echo the comments of one respondent, who wrote, "I think more emphasis needs to be placed on the person's ability to perform all duties assigned rather than gender. If a person can handle a position and desires to do it, they should be given the opportunity."

The second arrangement that will improve the ability of women to participate on equal terms with men is the repeal of the law prohibiting the participation of lesbians and gay men in the U.S. military. It is painfully apparent that this ban hurts many lesbians and gay men. Many wish to serve in the military but know that to do so is not without risk. Many do join the military, only to have their careers ended prematurely.

But, as I have illustrated, the ban on lesbians and gay men also impacts negatively on all women, regardless of sexual orientation. If the confirmation of heterosexuality were not imperative, women would be free to engage in a much wider range of behaviors, particularly those labeled masculine. But, equally important, if women did not feel compelled to insure that they are seen as heterosexual, there would be less pressure to enact femininity, a marker of heterosexuality. By having to confirm heterosexuality, women enact femininity, thereby insuring that they will be perceived as less capable than their male counterparts. The link between gender and sexuality situated in an institution that formally regulates sexuality insures the subordination of women. To eliminate such formal regulation would greatly enhance opportunities for the more equal participation of women.

The story presented here is not intended to be a sad tale of women's secondary status and failure to overcome. In fact, many of the comments offered by the women in this study attest to their dedication and success in light of the barriers with which they were confronted. Consider the woman who wrote, "Although I experienced many problems because I was female in the military, I think it is only fair to say that it was probably the most interesting and exciting time of my life." Women who have participated, and continue to participate, in the U.S. military have always faced challenges to their participation. For the most part, their story is one of victory.

This book, however, is not about individual successes or even the overwhelming success of women as a group. It is about barriers to women's participation in the military and how women negotiate these barriers. It offers an examination of what these processes contribute to our understanding of gender as dynamic rather than static, as well as the relationship between gender and sexuality. By understanding how gender is produced at the interactional level, how the interactional level is related to existing institutional arrangements, and how the link between gender and sexuality empowers this relationship, we can offer a new vision for the equal participation of women and men in the military and, more important, throughout society.

METHODOLOGICAL
APPENDIX

Research that addresses women in the military reflects a wide variety of methodological approaches. The literature includes small qualitative studies (Dunivin 1988; Schneider and Schneider 1988; Williams 1989), large quantitative studies (Hosek and Peterson 1990; Segal 1978), oral histories (Marshall 1987), and autobiographies (Barkalow 1990). Stiehm (1989) completed hundreds of personal interviews and utilized the quantitative research, documents, and policies of governmental agencies to tell the story of enlisted women in today's military. While the variety of methods is due in part to the specific goals of the research, like most research it is also due to differences in resources, access, and expertise. However, one's choice of methodology is also affected by the specific topic of study. Even if one had all the resources, access, and expertise necessary, there are certain topics regarding the military on which it would remain difficult to conduct research. Gender and sexuality are among these topics.

There is no doubt that the military is concerned with appearances. Senior members of the military have readily admitted that one of their concerns about allowing lesbians and gay men, especially gay men, to be "open" is the effect they believe this would have on public perceptions of the military. For many reasons, as political as they are emotional, the military has a stake in how it is perceived. Military personnel have been strongly advised against talking to the media about a number of issues (e.g., Desert Storm, gays in the military, Tailhook). If individuals choose to do so, it is made clear that they must insure that no one thinks they are talking on behalf of the military. There is a fine line between the First Amendment and insubordination. This is particularly true for personnel who may wish to provide accounts of the role of women in the military. Women, whether enlisted or officer, need to be assured that talking with a researcher will not be held against them.

There are several ways to provide this assurance. If the goal of the research is likely to benefit the military, leaders will be less likely to fear negative repercussions. If one has plentiful resources, whether connections to military leadership or Congress, the military will likely be more receptive to the conduct of research. If one has documented expertise in the area and a reputation for research that does not malign the military, the same holds true. All of these factors are tied to access. Persons such as Charles Moskos, David Segal, Mady Wechsler Segal, and Judith Stiehm have all of these attributes. The fact that at least three of these people were invited to testify before the Senate Armed Services Committee hearings on gays in the military attests to their status and reputation; it is likely that they could undertake research on more sensitive gender issues without being perceived as a threat. Moskos, in fact, has claimed that his work includes "the most extensive survey taken on gender issues in the military" (1993: 1). Such research could not have been undertaken without an established record of scholarship and support for the military.

The issues are different, and more complex, when we turn to the subject of sexuality. Whether we are talking about sexuality in general or homosexuality in particular, the military, like society in general, has reasons to suppress such inquiry. In fact, upon receiving the results of a study it commissioned on gays in the military, the Pentagon refused to disseminate the findings because they were not what the leadership had hoped to see. Only when the information was leaked did the public become aware of the findings (Dyer 1990).

If the military, as an institution, has reasons to stifle discussions about sexuality, individual members of the military have an even greater reason to do so. This is particularly true if one is lesbian, gay, or bisexual or is at risk for being labeled as such. To my knowledge, no quantitative study of women veterans and women in the military has included identification of the respondents' sexual orientation. Oral histories have done so, many using pseudonyms, but nothing appears to exist that includes such information in a quantitative data set. The degree of fear among women in the military and, interestingly, among women veterans is such that to provide this information presents two specific difficulties. The first is the locating of participants. The second is the ability to assure participants that their anonymity will be maintained. While women on active duty worry, justifiably so, that they will be discharged if they are identified as lesbian or bisexual, women veterans worry that they might lose their benefits if this information is revealed. Others remain on reserve status and are therefore subject to the Uniform Code of Military Justice and federal law, which prohibit sodomy and homosexuality, respectively.

Even heterosexual women might have reason to shy away from inquiry about sexuality in general. The degree to which women in the military have been maligned around issues of their sexuality (i.e., sexual availability, the focus on their sex rather than their competence) makes them understandably skeptical of such inquiry. In addition, we live in a society that, while it is obsessed with sex (e.g., film, rock videos, advertising), exhibits an almost puritanical attitude of "do it if you must, but don't talk about it." All of these factors add to the difficulty in conducting research on gender and sexuality among women in the military.

It was not possible to locate a random sample of women veterans or women in the military. In 1985 the Veterans Administration sought to obtain a random sample of women veterans. To gather a sample of 3,003 women veterans, they made 526,367 telephone calls to households in the United States (Veterans Administration 1985). There are no accurate sampling frames of women veterans from which to draw a random sample. This is even more true when the parameters of eligibility are service during or since a particular time. Thus, random, or even probability, sampling was not an option.

I chose, by necessity, to attempt to identify potential respondents through a variety of avenues. I posted notices at women's bookstores, gay and lesbian community centers, on computer bulletin boards, in publications such as *Minerva's Bulletin Board* and *The Register* (the newsletter of the Women in Military Service for America Project), and at college and university veterans program offices around the nation. A total

of about 500 surveys were distributed; 394 were completed
and returned. This provides a response rate of about 79 percent. Due to cost, no follow-up procedure was implemented
to increase the response rate.

In order to have been eligible to participate in this research,
respondents had to have served at least one year of active duty
in the United States armed forces some time since 1976. This
includes attendance at a service academy. These two requirements, "one year of active duty" and "since 1976," were for-
mulated for specific reasons.

Most military personnel spend a minimum of three months
completing their initial entry training. I wanted to insure that
respondents had spent at least a minimum amount of time in
the environment of the military, both in training and in permanent duty station assignments. Training settings are radi-
cally different from permanent duty stations. The rules tend to
be more tightly enforced, relationships among trainees are
more controlled, and trainees have little to no interaction with
the world outside their unit. This is a period of resocialization
in which the trainee could be said to not yet have entered the
"real military." My goal was to insure that respondents had
spent time in the day-to-day world of the "real military."

The 1970s were full of changes for the U.S. military, particularly for women in the military. In 1972 women were first
permitted to participate in the Reserve Officers Training
Corps, the training mechanism for military officers that operates in conjunction with colleges and universities around the
nation. In 1973 the draft was abolished, resulting in an increased need for the enlistment of women. The Vietnam War
is considered to have ended in 1975, leading to the need to

adapt to peacetime operations. In 1976 the first women were permitted to enter the service academies (e.g., West Point). Nontraditional career fields, previously closed to women, were becoming available to military women. In 1978 the Women's Army Corps was permanently disbanded, "WAC" battalions began to train men, and women entered units that had been largely male. These changes occurred at different times across branches, but, regardless of branch, the 1970s were a time of radical change throughout the military of the United States.

The focus of this research is how the experiences of women in the military have been mediated by gender and sexuality, specifically as related to their serving with men. Prior to the dissolution of the women's branches (e.g., the Women's Army Corps), women worked with men but had separate regulations, chains of command, and quarters. Once women and men were integrated into the same "branch" (e.g., the United States Army), they not only worked together in much greater numbers but were in the same units, held the same jobs, and were subject to the same policies. These changes created an entirely different experience for the women who served in the "integrated" military, as opposed to those who had served when women and men were largely segregated.

Given that the focus of this research is on the experience of women in the male-dominated world of the military, I wanted to hear from those women who had served in the military in which women and men served together. To that end, I chose 1976 as a pivotal year. Any woman who has served since 1976 undoubtedly served in an environment that was much more sex-integrated. It is these experiences that I wished to examine. It should be noted, however, that men who serve in the combat arms continue to serve in a highly sex-segregated military.

In addition to identifying respondents with regard to time and length of service, I also wished to obtain a sample that was approximately half lesbian and bisexual and half heterosexual. I sought to do this because I believed there was a good possibility that experiences would differ on the basis of the sexual orientation of the respondents. Oversampling for lesbian and bisexual women would allow me to make such comparisons.

Although the overall sample contained 394 women, the data presented here are based on the surveys of the 285 women who were retained in the sample when I utilized logistic regression, a procedure in which cases with missing data "drop out" of the analysis. For consistency across the analyses, I used that same sample in the cross-tabulations as well.

I sought to collect data via a questionnaire for several reasons. First, it would allow me to get a lot of information in a systematic fashion. Second, it would allow me to collect data anonymously. The latter was of particular concern for reasons previously addressed. Third, unlike interviews, the completion of questionnaires would allow respondents time to think about their experiences and how they wanted to express themselves. Finally, the questionnaires would provide me with information to use in structuring the subset of interviews that I planned to do later in the research process. The questionnaire data were collected from 1993 to 1995. In 1996 I conducted interviews with women in Tucson, Seattle, and Minneapolis, primarily to give them an opportunity to comment on my findings and to offer additional narrative remarks.

The fifteen-page questionnaire contains seven sections that include yes/no questions, multiple-choice questions, open-ended questions, check-off items, and Likert-scale items. Each section has a different focus. A pretest with nine respondents was conducted. In addition to having these nine individuals complete the survey, I met with two of them to discuss any problems or suggestions that they wished to address. The results of the pretest indicated that few changes were needed. I also made a point of asking respondents to keep track of how long they spent completing the questionnaire and whether they thought it was too long. Only one respondent thought it was too long, but the section she advised cutting could not be cut without substantially altering the focus of the data collection.

The sections of the questionnaire are as follow: 1) personal information, 2) military service, 3) education, 4) personal assessment, 5) personal resources, 6) gender, and 7) sexuality. *Personal information* includes demographic information such as date of birth, occupation, and military service of parent/guardian. *Military service* includes, for example, dates and branch of service, reasons for leaving the service, and type of discharge. *Education* requests information about both military and civilian education. The *personal assessment* section is aimed at determining respondents' assessment of their military experience with regard to, for example, stress, job performance, physical fitness, and sexual harassment. The *personal resources* section is aimed at determining respondents' assessment of activities that may have provided various types of support, such as sports or family, as well as other responses to stress such as alcohol or drug use. This section also includes assessment of strategies around gender and sexuality. The *gender* section asks respondents to indicate beliefs and attitudes about issues of femininity and masculinity, particularly with regard to the role that gender might play in their participation as women in the military. Finally, the section that addresses *sexuality* focuses on both the sexual orientation of the respondent and her attitudes about homosexuality. Following this section, a few items were added that ask the respondents about their experiences as veterans.

Two versions of the questionnaire were produced. In the *gender* section, the items on femininity and masculinity were in one order on Form A and in the reverse order on Form B. If all questionnaires had asked, for example, all of the questions about femininity first, there was the possibility of having a biased instrument. If Form A and Form B were distributed randomly, roughly half of the respondents should have completed questionnaires with items ordered one way and the other half forms with the other order. In fact, 50.2 percent of the respondents completed Form A and 49.8 percent completed Form B. While this process made distribution of the survey more difficult (e.g., I did not allow people to photocopy their survey for distribution), I believe it provides greater integrity to the quality of the data and significantly reduces the likelihood of bias based on item order within the questionnaire.

Although the question that lies at the heart of this research is about strategies, there are other questions that must be answered in order to examine some basic assertions about women's participation in the military. I was first interested in determining whether women felt that a penalty existed for those perceived as too feminine or too masculine. If women did not perceive the existence of penalties, one might question whether there would be any need for strategizing. If, on the other hand, women believed that there were penalties for being perceived as too masculine or too feminine, it would not be surprising that they might develop and employ strategies to avoid such perceptions. I asked the following questions: 1) Do you think that there are penalties for military women who may be perceived as being too feminine? and 2) Do you think that there are penalties for military women who may be perceived as being too masculine?

The questions of perceptions of femininity and masculinity are aimed at determining whether perceptions of gender may play a role in the participation of women in the military. The follow-up questions continue in that vein but edge toward the subject of sexuality. Respondents who indicated that they did believe such penalties existed were asked to describe what those penalties might be. It is this information that I believed would begin to illustrate the connection between gender and sexuality, particularly how sexuality is used to enforce the gender rules. Questions about femininity and masculinity are used to establish a foundation from which I argue that ideas about gender and sexuality are important factors in the ability of women to participate in the male-dominated world of the military.

Having addressed the topic of how women perceive gender and sexuality as being linked to their role as women in the military, I turned to the subject of strategies. If women do have to balance their femininity and masculinity and if sexuality can be used, whether by the women or by others, to maintain or disrupt that balance, how do women successfully manage both gender and sexuality? The survey raised questions of strategies by listing twenty-eight behaviors in which respondents may or may not have engaged. Such behaviors included, but were not limited to, "I usually wear makeup on duty," "I preferred low quarters to pumps," or "When I had a boyfriend, I made sure people knew it" (see the survey for all possible responses). Without reference to strategizing, the questionnaire stated: "The following items pertain to your behavior while on active duty. Check any of the following that you believe applied to yourself." There were two separate follow-up questions to this section. The first asked, "Do you believe that any of those behaviors checked were part of a conscious attempt to insure that others perceived you as feminine? as masculine?" I then asked, in two separate questions, "Are there other things that you did that you believe were a conscious attempt to insure that others perceived you as 'feminine?' as 'masculine?' It should be noted that I was particularly interested in *conscious* strategies as a means of distinguishing between expressive behaviors for which many women, accurate or not, would feel there was no underlying motivation. Finally, I asked, again in two separate questions, "Are there other things that you did to make yourself feel more feminine/masculine of which others were unaware?" Another question asked, "Do you believe that any of those behaviors checked were part of a conscious attempt to avoid being suspected of being lesbian/bisexual?"

This section served three purposes. First, it would provide some quantitative information about the types of strategies, if any, that were employed. Second, it provided me with information with which to guide later interviews. That is, rather than beginning "cold," I could ask interviewees to elaborate on a particular response. Third, it provided a source for open-ended questions about other strategies that women used so that I could create a more comprehensive list of such strategies.

Other questions focus on relationships between other variables (i.e., demographic and attitudinal) and those described earlier. For example, does perception of the existence of penalties vary by sexual orientation? Does the type of penalty described vary by sexual orientation? Does military rank correlate with perceptions of the importance of gender perceptions? Questions such as these enabled me elaborate as to whether women experience the military differently on the basis of other characteristics.

These questions, taken together, allowed me to explore a world in which gender and sexuality intersect to create a mechanism by which the participation of women in the military may be controlled by the institution as well as by their peers.

The analysis of the quantitative data relied on a variety of statistical methods. Analysis of the foundational questions about pressure to act in a particular way and questions about the penalties for "gender deviance" utilized cross-tabulations with the Chi-square statistic. A more detailed analysis of these relationships involved the use of several logistic regression analyses, with the belief in the existence of pressures and penalties and employment of strategies serving as dependent variables. There are several ways in which these questions might be examined. In each model I included a variety of independent variables including, but not limited to, branch, rank, sexual orientation, education, and time in service.

In addition to statistical analyses, I performed content analyses on the open-ended items that asked respondents to provide information about additional strategies. From these analyses I not only gained information about what strategies women recognized themselves as employing but also gained information that helped me develop a typology of strategies for the management of gender.

The combination of quantitative and qualitative data provides not only information about statistical relationships but also detailed information about the substance of these relationships. It is one thing to say that, for example, a particular number of women felt that women are penalized for being perceived as "too feminine." It is quite another to be able to say what the penalties were and how women avoided them. The dual nature of data collection allowed me to delve further into the "facts" and to examine more closely the often hidden relationships between those "facts" and gender ideology.

Although cross-tabulations are informative and interesting, they do not, in all likelihood, tell the whole story. To try to capture a more complete picture, I conducted logistic regression analyses with different dependent variables. By doing so I wished to examine the net effects of different variables. That is, would relationships observed in cross-tabulations hold up when controls were entered into the equation? Each regression contained sixteen independent variables.

Some were of substantive interest; others were primarily control variables. Eleven other independent variables were included as controls.

Three of these variables were standard demographic variables representing current age (AGE), race (RACED), and civilian education at the time the respondent first entered active duty (CIVEDBEG). A respondent's race was coded as white/nonwhite. A second age variable reflected the age of the respondent at the time she first entered active duty (AGEATAD). It is possible that a woman's experience with the military could differ significantly if she entered the military at age eighteen as opposed to twenty-five. Women have traditionally entered the military at a slightly older age than men. This has, however, changed over time, and I felt it important to control for any differences in the sample that may have occurred because of a variable level of maturity or life experience at the point one entered the military.

Other variables reflected the first year in which the respondent entered the military (FIRSTMIL), the last year in which the respondent served on active duty (LASTAD), the number of years of active duty service (YEARSAD), and a dummy variable for whether the respondent is currently on active duty (MILSTAT). Because the role of women both in the military and in society has changed so dramatically over the past several decades, I wanted to be able to control for any effects of having entered the service during a particular period. For example, a woman who entered the military in 1964 would, arguably, have had a qualitatively different experience than a woman who first entered the military in 1988. Not only were there fewer women, but the military was organized differently, as well. Prior to the mid-1970s women served in a more auxiliary fashion.

A similar argument can be made for the last year served. If experiences are different by period, then a woman who left the service in the mid-1970s might have a very different recollection from a woman who left the service in 1992. I also felt it important to control for the number of years served. Someone who served three years has a more limited frame of reference than someone who served twenty years. Unfortunately, if there is any effect of years served, I have been unable to isolate the underlying meaning of such an effect. If, for example, women with more time served have a more positive assessment of their service, I cannot speculate as to whether this means that because they had fewer problems they stayed in, whereas women who encountered more problems got out, or whether anyone who stays in longer inevitably becomes more assimilated into the military. That is, would those who served fewer years have indicated more positive attitudes had they stayed in? Although I cannot make such a determination, controlling for number of years served is important nonetheless. Finally, it is quite possible that women who are still on active duty would have different opinions from women who are no longer on active duty. Some difference might be expected for reasons similar to those just described. In addition, it is quite possible that while one is participating in an activity, one is likely to view that experience less critically than might be the case when she is no longer participating.

Also included was a variable reflecting the respondent's agreement with the statement(s) "I would describe myself as feminine/masculine" (YOUFEM/YOUMASC). I felt it important to have some assessment of how the respondents viewed themselves in terms of gender. Finally, another variable indicates whether the respondent heard about the study from a veteran or a nonveteran contact (CONTACT). In designing the research, I found it necessary to identify routes by which a broad range of participants could be identified. I knew that one major source of participation would be a large, national project on women veterans; other sources included women's bookstores and lesbian networks. Because of the possibility that the identity "veteran" would be more salient for those contacted via a veteran's project, I thought it wise to control for the possibility of having two somewhat different "samples" within the sample.

Each regression is weighted such that officers "count less." The sample of 285 women contained 184 enlisted personnel (65 percent) and 101 officers (35 percent), or an overrepresentation of officers. Of all women currently on active duty, 16 percent are officers. Thus, the sample contains more than twice as many officers as would be reflective of the current distribution. Because of this, I weighted the sample so that it was more representative of the rank distribution among women in the military. The difficulty was in determining which number to use to create the weight. The percentage of all women who were officers varied a great deal between the years 1976 and 1994. The numbers also vary across branch and specific rank. After examining the periods of time in which most respondents served and the available data for these periods, I chose 12 percent as representative of the percentage of all women who were officers. Using this figure, I was able to create a weight for officers that would artificially suppress their representation in the regression models, but would not change the number of cases for significance tests. That is, weights were assigned such that, after weighting, 12 percent of the sample was officers, and the average weight was 1.

The first rank variable (RANKEO) categorizes respondents on the basis of whether they are enlisted or officer. It should be noted again that all measures of rank are based on the highest rank attained. The sample contains 184 enlisted personnel and 101 officers. When weighted, representation was 242 enlisted personnel and 44 officers. The weighting results in an "artificial" sample size of 286, thus the extra case.

The second variable (RANKJS) categorizes a respondent by whether she is "junior" or "senior." A junior service member is one who is either junior enlisted (E1–E4) or junior (i.e., company grade) officer (O1–O3). They are the personnel who have served the least time, may not have career intentions, and have the least power compared to others of their rank category. Included in this category are Warrant Officers and midshipmen (*sic*) who participated in the study. A senior service member is either a noncommissioned officer (E5–E9) or a senior (i.e., field grade) officer (O4–O6). There were no flag officers (i.e., generals or admirals) in the sample. There were 164 junior and 121 senior respondents. When weighted, cross-tabulation representation was 158 junior and 128 senior respondents. This is likely due to the very high number of junior officers who participated in the study. Weighting the officers to "count for less" would mean "fewer" junior officers, which would, in turn, reduce the number of junior respondents.

The third variable of interest is sexual orientation. The sample contains 212 women who identify as heterosexual and 73 who identify as lesbian or bisexual. When weighted by rank, representation is 204 heterosexual women and 82 who identify as lesbian or bisexual. Although I have data on the respondent's self-identification when entering the service, when leaving, and currently, I chose to use current identification. I did so because I believe that, even though the data are retrospective, it is one's current identification that most influences how respondents view or recall experiences. It should also be noted that answers to open-ended questions show that some of the bisexual women are currently married to men.

The methodological problems of sexual orientation highlight the behavior-versus-identity debate and the difficulties in determining one's "true" sexual orientation. I have used what I feel represents military guidelines. I am interested not in sexual acts but in how an individual identifies herself. Further, I collapse lesbian and bisexual into one category for reasons of sample size and because the military treats them the same. Thus, while I acknowledge the contentiousness of the issue, I do use the binary categories of heterosexual versus lesbian/bisexual because of their utility to this project.

One major shortcoming of this sample is the underrepresentation of women of color. Although the number of women of color in the 1970s in the military was far smaller than it is now, the number of women of color in the military today demands that they be represented in any research on women in the military. Of all women in the military, 42.8 percent are women of color. This sample contains twenty-eight, or 9.8 percent, women of color. Some of this can be explained by the fact that there are far more women veterans who are white, and I was "sampling" all women who have served since 1976, not just those who are currently on active duty. But, even taking that into account, the numbers are lower than they should be. There is any number of possible explanations, none of which I can confirm. My best guess is that the identity "women veteran" may be more salient for white women. This, in and of itself, would be an important piece of information to verify. In the end, I can only suggest that these findings can best be generalized to white women veterans and that the experiences of military women of color may be different.

In what follows I present the results of the logistic regression models examining pressures, penalties, and strategies. Following those tables is the survey that was used to collect the data. I have not provided an interview schedule because the interviews were conducted in an unstructured fashion.

TABLE 1
Results from Logistic Multiple Regression Models Predicting
Beliefs about Military Pressure to Act Feminine or Masculine

	DEPENDENT VARIABLE			
	Pressure to Act Feminine		Pressure to Act Masculine	
	INDEPENDENT VARIABLES			
	Estimate	Prob Chi-Sq	Estimate	Prob Chi-Sq
AGE	-0.2184	.1653	-0.0887	.4278
RACED	0.4435	.3471	0.4412	.3092
FIRSTMIL	-0.2045	.2126	-0.1248	.3038
AGEATAD	0.1660	.3138	0.0190	.8734
YEARSAD	0.0172	.8284	-0.0438	.4858
LASTAD	-0.0499	.5218	0.0829	.1819
AIR	0.5144	.1305	-1.0949	.0014**
RANKEO	-0.2249	.7130	0.7112	.1859
RANKJS	0.4580	.2615	-0.8950	.0158*
MILSTAT	0.0708	.8917	-0.4348	.3567
CIVEDBEG	0.1746	.2991	-0.2698	.1029
MILJOB	-0.1504	.7517	0.3278	.4164
YOUFEM	0.4042	.3210	0.0505	.8862
YOUMASC	1.3649	.0011**	0.0650	.8742
SOCURR	1.4899	.0004***	0.7467	.0674
CONTACT	0.0111	.9785	0.9996	.0099**

p = .05 *
p = .01 **
p = .001 ***
(two-tailed tests)

TABLE 2
*Results from Logistic Multiple Regression Models Predicting
Beliefs about Penalties for Being Perceived as
Too Feminine or Too Masculine*

	DEPENDENT VARIABLE			
	Penalties for Femininity		*Penalties for Masculinity*	
	INDEPENDENT VARIABLES			
	Estimate	Prob Chi-Sq	Estimate	Prob Chi-Sq
AGE	0.1910	.1547	0.0146	.8800
RACED	0.9341	.0682	0.3669	.4329
FIRSTMIL	0.0774	.5874	-0.0318	.7694
AGEATAD	-0.1837	.1901	-0.00884	.9319
YEARSAD	-0.1777	.0166*	-0.0199	.7418
LASTAD	0.1229	.0898	0.0257	.6646
AIR	-0.7610	.0134*	-0.7580	.0121*
RANKEO	1.2402	.0317*	0.9239	.0795
RANKJS	-0.8547	.0155*	-0.8036	.0208*
MILSTAT	0.2904	.5363	-0.2072	.6384
CIVEDBEG	-0.2981	.0660	-0.1718	.2372
MILJOB	-0.5108	.1905	0.2753	.4658
YOUFEM	-0.2777	.4324	-0.2410	.4869
YOUMASC	-0.3581	.4015	0.1706	.6925
SOCURR	0.2290	.5789	1.6152	.0002***
CONTACT	-0.3115	.4091	0.3154	.3958

p = .05 *
p = .01 **
p = .001 ***
(two-tailed tests)

TABLE 3
Results from Logistic Multiple Regression Models Predicting
the Employment of Strategies for Femininity or Masculinity

	DEPENDENT VARIABLE			
	Strategies *for* *Femininity*		*Strategies* *for* *Masculinity*	
	INDEPENDENT VARIABLES			
		Prob		Prob
	Estimate	Chi-Sq	Estimate	Chi-Sq
AGE	-0.0544	.5671	-0.1403	.3905
RACED	0.2434	.5646	0.2845	.6258
FIRSTMIL	-0.0930	.3797	-0.0252	.8983
AGEATAD	-0.00212	.9835	-0.1190	.5144
YEARSAD	-0.0717	.2277	0.0353	.8288
LASTAD	0.0990	.0889	-0.0657	.6813
AIR	-0.4908	.1113	0.0785	.8659
RANKEO	0.3974	.4197	1.3309	.0864
RANKJS	-0.4596	.1857	-0.4261	.4508
MILSTAT	-0.5524	.2194	-0.0550	.9360
CIVEDBEG	-0.0178	.9029	0.0717	.7628
MILJOB	0.0758	.8443	-0.5862	.4298
YOUFEM	0.9617	.0074**	-0.0237	.9637
YOUMASC	0.4040	.3104	1.6991	.0008***
SOCURR	0.1373	.7178	-0.2863	.6231
CONTACT	-0.0357	.9178	-0.4662	.3590

p = .05 *
p = .01 **
p = .001 ***
(two-tailed tests)

WOMEN VETERANS STUDY

This survey is designed to gather information about your experiences in the United States military. For the purposes of the questions contained within this survey, "active duty" is defined as a period of active duty service of at least six months in length. All information is confidential.

Personal Information

1. Date of birth: Month _____ Day _____ Year _____

2. Race/ethnicity:
   _____ 1. African-American
   _____ 2. Asian
   _____ 3. Caucasian, not Hispanic
   _____ 4. Hispanic
   _____ 5. Native American
   _____ 6. Pacific Islander
   _____ 7. Other (indicate) _____

3. Which category best describes the type of **paid** work you are doing now?

(If currently on active duty check the category that best describes the type of work you do within the military and note "military" next to your answer.)

____ 1. Professional/Technical

____ 2. Management/Administration

____ 3. Clerical

____ 4. Sales

____ 5. Skilled Trades

____ 6. Unskilled Labor

____ 7. Service Worker

____ 8. Farmer

____ 9. Other (describe) _____

____ 10. None/Not Applicable (includes students and homemakers)

What is your occupation? _____

4. If you were living with a male parent/guardian at the time you left high school, which category best describes the type of **paid** work he was doing at that time?

____ 1. Professional/Technical

____ 2. Management/Administration

____ 3. Clerical

____ 4. Sales

____ 5. Skilled Trades

____ 6. Unskilled Labor

____ 7. Service Worker

____ 8. Farmer

____ 9. Other (describe) _____

____ 10. None/Not Applicable (includes students and homemakers)

What was his occupation at that time? _____

5. If you were living with a female parent/guardian at the time you left high school, which category best describes the type of **paid** work she was doing at that time?
  ____ 1. Professional/Technical
  ____ 2. Management/Administration
  ____ 3. Clerical
  ____ 4. Sales
  ____ 5. Skilled Trades
  ____ 6. Unskilled Labor
  ____ 7. Service Worker
  ____ 8. Farmer
  ____ 9. Other (describe) _____
  ____ 10. None/Not Applicable (includes students and homemakers)

What was her occupation at that time? _____

6. Did either of your parents/guardians ever serve in the military?
  Yes ____ No ____ Don't Know ____

7. If yes, did they serve at any time after your birth?
  Yes ____ No ____ Don't Know ____
  Not Applicable ____

8. At the time you first entered the military did you have a spouse/partner or close friend who was or had been in the military?

Yes _____ No _____

9. Which of the following best describes the location in which you were living during most of your high school years?

_____ 1. In open country, but not on a farm

_____ 2. On a farm

_____ 3. In a small city/town (under 50,000) not near large city

_____ 4. In a medium size city/town (50,000–250,000) not near large city

_____ 5. In a suburb near a large city

_____ 6. In a large city (over 250,000)

_____ 7. Don't know

Military Service

10. On what date, as closely as you can recall, did you first join the military? This would be the date that you first signed up (e.g., Delayed Entry Program, joined a Reserve unit, etc.).

Month _____ Day _____ Year _____

11. What was your age when you first began active duty of any kind? _____

12. First tour of active duty of at least six months:

Date entered active duty: Month _____ Year _____
Date departed active duty: Month _____ Year _____
(Leave date departed blank if you have remained on active duty.)

13. Was the **majority** of your active duty time spent:
    In the United States _____ Outside the U.S./At sea _____

14. Branch of service for period listed in item 12 above:
    _____ 1. Army
    _____ 2. Air Force
    _____ 3. Marines
    _____ 4. Navy

15. What was your pay grade when you **first** entered active duty? _____

16. What was your pay grade when you **last** departed active duty? _____
(If on active duty, indicate current grade.)

17. If you served any additional periods of active duty that were at least six months in length, please provide date and branch information below:

_____

18. What is your current military status?
    _____ 1. None
    _____ 2. Member of reserve unit
    _____ 3. Member of inactive reserve, not retired

_____ 4. Active

_____ 5. Retired

_____ 6. Not sure

19. If you checked 2, 3, 4 or 5 in item 18 above, what is your **current** pay grade? _____

20. Are you currently enrolled in ROTC?
Yes _____ No _____

21. Do you belong to any veteran/military organizations?
Yes _____ No _____

22. Please list all military awards you received **while on active duty**: (e.g., Army Commendation Medal, Good Conduct Medal, etc.)

_____

_____

_____

Thinking back to your longest tour of active duty, what were the **three** most important reasons for leaving? In the space below check off the three most important reasons for leaving active duty. If you are still on active duty, skip to item 49 below.

_____ 23. low pay

_____ 24. better civilian job opportunities

_____ 25. reduction in military benefits

_____ 26. quality of military personnel

_____ 27. unable to practice my job skills

_____ 28. bored with my job

_____ 29. did not like my job

_____ 30. wanted to get my civilian education

_____ 31. not eligible to reenlist/forced out

_____ 32. tired of barracks life

_____ 33. disliked location of assignments

_____ 34. didn't get the training I wanted

_____ 35. had to move too often

_____ 36. disliked being separated from my family

_____ 37. my family wanted me to leave the service

_____ 38. disagreed with personnel policies

_____ 39. the way the military treats members of my race/ethnic group

_____ 40. the way the military treats women

_____ 41. the way the military discriminates on the basis of rank

_____ 42. pregnancy

_____ 43. nobody tried to get me to stay

_____ 44. end of reserve tour/no chance to remain active

_____ 45. retired

_____ 46. other (describe) _____

47. If you checked item 31 (not eligible to reenlist/forced out) above, please describe the situation to which you are referring:

_____

_____

_____

48. If you checked item 38 (disagreed with personnel policies) above, please describe to which policies you are referring:

_____

_____

_____

49. Overall, how would you describe your military ratings/evaluations?

_____ 1. Poor

_____ 2. Fair

_____ 3. Average

_____ 4. Good

_____ 5. Excellent

50. How accurately do you believe your military ratings/evaluations reflected your performance?

_____ 1. Not at all accurately

_____ 2. Somewhat accurately

_____ 3. Accurately

If you checked 1 or 2 in item 50 above, why do you believe you were not evaluated accurately?

_____

_____

_____

51. What type of discharge did you last receive?

_____ 1. Honorable

_____ 2. General, under honorable conditions

_____ 3. Less than honorable

_____ 4. Other (describe) _____

_____ 5. Not applicable

Education

52. For which military jobs (e.g., clerk typist, military police, truck driver, data processor, pilot, etc.) did you received military training?

_____

_____

_____

53. What was your civilian education when you **first** entered active duty?

_____ 1. Some high school

_____ 2. Completed GED

_____ 3. High school diploma

_____ 4. Some college

_____ 5. Associate's degree

_____ 6. Bachelor's degree

_____ 7. Master's degree

_____ 8. Other (indicate) _____

54. What was your civilian education when you **last** departed active duty? (Leave blank if currently on active duty.)

_____ 1. Some high school

_____ 2. Completed GED

_____ 3. High school diploma

_____ 4. Some college

____ 5. Associate's degree

____ 6. Bachelor's degree

____ 7. Master's degree

____ 8. Other (indicate) _____

55. What is your civilian education at the current time?

____ 1. Some high school

____ 2. Completed GED

____ 3. High school diploma

____ 4. Some college

____ 5. Associate's degree

____ 6. Bachelor's degree

____ 7. Master's degree

____ 8. Other (indicate) _____

Personal Assessment

Except where otherwise indicated please use the scale below and select the one answer that **best** describes your opinion about the following issues. When answering, think about your active duty service overall, rather than focusing on one particular assignment. If you are still on active duty answer according to your assessment of your active duty service overall.

SD   Strongly Disagree

D   Disagree

U   Uncertain

A   Agree

SA   Strongly Agree

56. I think that my male coworkers thought I did my job as well as they did.

SD   D   U   A   SA

57. I think that my female coworkers thought I did my job as well as they did.

SD   D   U   A   SA

58. I think that my supervisors thought I performed my job as well as others they supervised in that position.

SD   D   U   A   SA

59. I think that I performed my job as well as my coworkers.

SD   D   U   A   SA

60. I think that I performed my job better than my coworkers.

SD   D   U   A   SA

61. Overall, I got along well with my coworkers.

SD   D   U   A   SA

62. I often felt stressed by the demands of my job.

SD   D   U   A   SA

63. I often felt that my pay was not sufficient to meet my expenses.

SD   D   U   A   SA

64. I often wished that the people in my unit got along better.

SD   D   U   A   SA

65. I often wished I had never joined the military.

SD   D   U   A   SA

66. I often felt that I could not really be myself while in the military.

SD   D   U   A   SA

67. I often felt a conflict between being a woman and being in the military.

SD   D   U   A   SA

68. I feel that my time in the military made me a better person.

SD   D   U   A   SA

69. I feel that the military interfered with my personal relationships.

SD   D   U   A   SA

70. I feel that the military encouraged me to make friends with those around me.

SD   D   U   A   SA

71. While on active duty my level of physical fitness was higher than usual.

SD   D   U   A   SA

72. I think that sexual harassment is a problem for most women in the military.

Yes _____ No _____

73. I believe that I was sexually harassed while in the military.

_____ 1. Definitely not true.

_____ 2. Probably not true.

_____ 3. Uncertain.

_____ 4. Probably true.

_____ 5. Definitely true.

If you answered probably true or definitely true to item 73, please describe the type of incident to which you are referring:

_____

_____

_____

_____

_____

_____

_____

74. I think that the military has done as much as they can to eliminate sexual harassment among service members.

Yes _____ No _____

75. Who do you think is more likely to experience sexual harassment in the military?

_____ 1. Women who are more feminine in appearance.

_____ 2. Women who are more masculine in appearance.

_____ 3. I don't think that women experience any more or less harassment than others on the basis of their "feminine" or "masculine" appearance.

_____ 4. I don't think any women really experience sexual harassment anymore.

76. I think that sex discrimination is a problem for most women in the military.

Yes _____ No _____

77. I believe that I was the victim of sex discrimination while in the military.

_____ 1. Definitely not true.

_____ 2. Probably not true.

_____ 3. Uncertain.

_____ 4. Probably true.

_____ 5. Definitely true.

If you answered probably true or definitely true to item 77, please describe the type of incident to which you are referring:

_____

_____

_____

_____

_____

_____

_____

_____

Personal Resources

Except where otherwise indicated please use the scale below and select the one answer that **best** describes your opinion about the following issues. When answering, think about your active duty service overall, rather than focusing on one particular assignment. If you are still on active duty answer according to your assessment of your active duty service overall.

SD   Strongly Disagree
D   Disagree
U   Uncertain
A   Agree
SA   Strongly Agree

78. I participated in organized, competitive team sports that were organized by the military.
    SD   D   U   A   SA

79. I participated in organized, competitive team sports that were organized by civilian organizations.
    SD   D   U   A   SA

80. I participated in organized, competitive individual sports that were organized by the military.
    SD   D   U   A   SA

81. I participated in organized, competitive individual sports that were organized by civilian organizations.
    SD   D   U   A   SA

82. I participated in informal team sports **on** post/base.

SD   D   U   A   SA

83. I participated in informal team sports **off** post/base.

SD   D   U   A   SA

84. I participated in informal individual sports **on** post/base.

SD   D   U   A   SA

85. I participated in informal individual sports **off** post/base.

SD   D   U   A   SA

86. I participated in hobbies (e.g., ceramics, photography, needlework, camping) **on** post/base.

SD   D   U   A   SA

87. I participated in hobbies (e.g., ceramics, photography, needlework, camping) **off** post/base.

SD   D   U   A   SA

88. I participated in **on** post/base groups with those who shared similar hobby interests (e.g., photography, travel, reading, computers).

SD   D   U   A   SA

89. I participated in **off** post/base groups with those who shared similar hobby interests (e.g., photography, travel, reading, computers).

SD   D   U   A   SA

90. I participated in **on** post/base groups with those who shared similar political interests (e.g., civil rights, animal rights, political clubs).

   SD   D   U   A   SA

91. I participated in **off** post/base groups with those who shared similar political interests (e.g., civil rights, animal rights, political clubs).

   SD   D   U   A   SA

92. I traveled for leisure whenever I could.

   SD   D   U   A   SA

93. In addition to required physical training, I worked out on my own (e.g., running, weight training, aerobics) to keep myself in shape.

   SD   D   U   A   SA

94. I kept a close watch on my diet so that I was "eating healthy."

   SD   D   U   A   SA

95. I made sure I got enough sleep whenever my schedule allowed.

   SD   D   U   A   SA

96. For emotional support I relied on close friends who were also in the military.

   SD   D   U   A   SA

97. For emotional support I relied on close friends who were not in the military.

SD   D   U   A   SA

98. I often relied on coworkers for emotional support.

SD   D   U   A   SA

99. I often relied on my family for emotional support.

SD   D   U   A   SA

100. I often relied on my spouse/partner for emotional support.

SD   D   U   A   SA

101. My religious/spiritual beliefs were a source of emotional support for me.

SD   D   U   A   SA

102. Organized religion was a source of emotional support for me.

SD   D   U   A   SA

103. I participated in voluntary military activities such as color guard, honor detail, unit councils, etc.

SD   D   U   A   SA

104. For me, the **one** most useful source of emotional support within the military was:

_____ 1. Chain of command (squad leader, commander, etc.)

____ 2. Chaplain or post/base religious organizations

____ 3. Military coworkers

____ 4. Military friends

____ 5. Other (please describe) _____

_____

105. For me, the **one** most useful source of emotional support outside the military was:

____ 1. Non-military friends

____ 2. Parents, siblings, children (**not** spouse/partner)

____ 3. Religion

____ 4. Spouse/Partner

____ 5. Other (please describe) _____

_____

106. I sought psychological counseling when I was on active duty.

Yes ____ No ____

107. Do you feel that your decision to seek counseling was related to your military service?

Yes ____ No ____ Uncertain ____

108. If you answered yes to item 107, why?

_____

_____

_____

109. If you sought counseling, were the counselors you saw:

Military ___ Civilian ___ Both ___ Not Applicable ___

110. Most of the time I was on active duty I smoked cigarettes:

_____ 1. Never

_____ 2. Sometimes, but less than a pack a day

_____ 3. About one pack a day

_____ 4. More than one pack a day

111. This was _____ than how much I smoked before I went on active duty.

More _____ Less _____ No different _____

112. If more or less, why do you think your smoking habits changed?

_____

113. The amount I smoked while on active duty was _____ than I now smoke.

More _____ Less _____ No different _____

114. Most of the time I was on active duty I drank alcoholic beverages:

_____ 1. Never

_____ 2. Only on occasion

_____ 3. 1 to 3 times a week

_____ 4. 4 to 6 times a week

_____ 5. Every day.

115. This was _____ than how much I drank before I went on active duty.

More _____ Less _____ No different _____

116. If more or less, why do you think your drinking habits changed?

_____

_____

117. The amount I drank while on active duty was _____ than I drink now.

More _____ Less _____ No different _____

118. Most of the time I was on active duty I used recreational drugs (hashish, marijuana, cocaine, amphetamines, etc.):

_____ 1. Never

_____ 2. Only on occasion

_____ 3. 1 to 3 times a week

_____ 4. 4 to 6 times a week

_____ 5. Every day.

119. This was _____ than how much I used before I went on active duty?

More _____ Less _____ No different _____

120. If more or less, why do you think your drug use changed?

_____

_____

121. The degree to which I used drugs while on active duty was _____ than I use now.

More _____ Less _____ No different _____

The following items pertain to your behavior while on active duty. Check any of the following that you believe applied to yourself:

_____ 122. I usually kept my fingernails polished.

_____ 123. I usually wore makeup on duty.

_____ 124. I usually wore makeup off duty.

_____ 125. I usually wore my hair long.

_____ 126. I wore cologne or perfume on duty.

_____ 127. When out of uniform I preferred to really "dress up."

_____ 128. I preferred to wear Class As or Class Bs whenever possible.

_____ 129. I preferred to wear a skirt uniform rather than pants.

_____ 130. I preferred pumps to low quarters.

_____ 131. I usually wore earrings when in Class As or Class Bs.

_____ 132. I preferred not to participate in "male" sports.

_____ 133. I did not want to be seen as "one of the guys."

_____ 134. I rarely wore makeup on duty.

_____ 135. I rarely wore makeup off duty.

_____ 136. I usually kept my hair trimmed above the collar.

_____ 137. When out of uniform I preferred to dress casually.

_____ 138. I preferred work uniforms to Class As or Class Bs.

_____ 139. I preferred to wear a pants uniform rather than a skirt.

_____ 140. I preferred low quarters to pumps.

_____ 141. I rarely wore earrings when in Class As or Class Bs.

_____ 142. I preferred to participate in "male" sports.

_____ 143. I wanted to be seen as "one of the guys."

_____ 144. I often socialized with the men in my unit.

_____ 145. I dated several of the men with whom I was stationed.

_____ 146. When I had a boyfriend, I made sure people knew it.

_____ 147. I got married while on active duty.

_____ 148. I was careful about with whom I was seen "hanging out."

_____ 149. I was careful about the places I "hung out."

150. Do you believe that any of those behaviors checked in items 122 to 149 were part of a conscious attempt to insure that others perceived you as "feminine"?

Yes _____ No _____

151. If yes, which behaviors (identify by item number):

_____

152. Are there other things that you did that you believe were a conscious attempt to insure that others perceived you as "feminine"?

Yes _____ No _____

If yes, please describe:

_____

_____

153. Are there other things that you did to make yourself feel more feminine but of which others were unaware?

Yes _____ No _____

If yes, please describe:

_____

_____

154. Do you believe that any of those behaviors checked in items 122 to 149 were part of a conscious attempt to insure that others perceived you as "masculine"?

Yes _____ No _____

155. If yes, which behaviors (identify by item number):

_____

156. Are there other things you did that were a conscious attempt to insure others perceived you as "masculine"?

Yes _____ No _____

If yes, please describe:

_____

_____

157. Are there other things that you did to make yourself feel more masculine but of which others were unaware?

Yes _____ No _____

If yes, please describe:

_____

Note: The next three items are to be completed by **all** respondents, regardless of sexual orientation.

158. Do you believe that any of those behaviors checked in items 122 to 149 were part of a conscious attempt to avoid being suspected of being lesbian/ bisexual?

Yes _____ No _____

159. If yes, which behaviors (identify by number):

_____

160. Are there other things that you did that you believe were a conscious effort to avoid being suspected of being lesbian/bisexual?

Yes _____ No _____

If yes, please describe:

_____

Gender

161. Would you describe yourself as feminine?
Yes _____ No _____

162. Do you think that the military pressures or encourages women in the military to "act feminine"?
Yes _____ No _____

163. Do you think that women can exercise power and authority while retaining their femininity?
Yes _____ No _____

164. Do you think that there are penalties for military women who may be perceived as being too feminine?

Yes _____ No _____

If yes, please give an example.

_____
_____
_____
_____
_____
_____
_____

165. Do you think that women in the military should do their best to eliminate their feminine qualities while on the job?

Yes _____ No _____

166. What does the term "feminine" mean to you?

_____
_____
_____
_____

167. Would you describe yourself as masculine?

Yes _____ No _____

168. Do you believe that the military pressures or encourages women in the military to "act masculine"?

Yes _____ No _____

169. Do you think that women can exercise power and authority without being perceived as too masculine?

Yes ____ No ____

170. Do you think that there are penalties for military women who may be perceived as being too masculine?

Yes ____ No ____

If yes, please give an example.

_____

_____

_____

_____

_____

_____

171. Do you think that women in the military should do their best to eliminate their masculine qualities while on the job?

Yes ____ No ____

172. Do you believe that women in other traditionally male occupations (e.g., law, the trades, business) are pressured by their peers to "act masculine"?

Yes ____ No ____

173. What does the term "masculine" mean to you?

_____

_____

_____

_____

174. Is there a conflict in your mind between being a woman and being a member of the military?

Yes _____ No _____

Sexuality

175. Thinking back to when you **first** entered active duty, what did you perceive your own sexual orientation to be?

_____ 1. Bisexual
_____ 2. Heterosexual
_____ 3. Lesbian
_____ 4. Uncertain

176. Thinking back to when you **first** entered active duty, what do you believe most of your coworkers perceived your sexual orientation to be?

_____ 1. Bisexual
_____ 2. Heterosexual
_____ 3. Lesbian

177. Thinking back to when you **last** departed active duty, what did you perceive your own sexual orientation to be? (If still on active duty, indicate what you currently perceive your own sexual orientation to be.)

_____ 1. Bisexual
_____ 2. Heterosexual
_____ 3. Lesbian
_____ 4. Uncertain

178. Thinking back to when you **last** departed active duty, what do you believe most of your coworkers perceived your

sexual orientation to be? (If still on active duty, indicate what you currently believe your coworkers perceptions to be.)

____ 1. Bisexual
____ 2. Heterosexual
____ 3. Lesbian

179. What do you consider your current sexual orientation to be?

____ 1. Bisexual
____ 2. Heterosexual
____ 3. Lesbian
____ 4. Uncertain

Note: The following four items are to be completed by **all** respondents, regardless of sexual orientation.

180. Other military personnel thought I was a lesbian.

____ 1. Definitely not true
____ 2. Probably not true
____ 3. Uncertain
____ 4. Probably true
____ 5. Definitely true

181. I was harassed because other military personnel thought I was a lesbian.

____ 1. Definitely not true
____ 2. Probably not true
____ 3. Uncertain
____ 4. Probably true
____ 5. Definitely true

182. I was investigated because of allegations of homosexuality.

_____ 1. Yes
_____ 2. No
_____ 3. Uncertain

183. Do you think that the ban on homosexuality in the military should be lifted?

Yes _____ No _____

If yes, why? If not, why not?

_____

_____

This section asks about other military personnel with whom you interacted while on active duty. Complete **only** the part that applies to you.

If you identified as lesbian/bisexual for **any** part of the time you were on active duty answer the following items, 184 to 188. If you identified **only** as heterosexual, skip to item 189 below.

184. Women who I believe were heterosexual knew that I was lesbian/bisexual.

_____ 1. Definitely not true
_____ 2. Probably not true
_____ 3. Uncertain
_____ 4. Probably true
_____ 5. Definitely true

185. Men who I believe were heterosexual knew that I was lesbian/bisexual.

_____ 1. Definitely not true

_____ 2. Probably not true

_____ 3. Uncertain

_____ 4. Probably true

_____ 5. Definitely true

186. Some of my supervisors knew that I was lesbian/bisexual.

_____ 1. Definitely not true

_____ 2. Probably not true

_____ 3. Uncertain

_____ 4. Probably true

_____ 5. Definitely true

187. If you answered probably true or definitely true to any of the previous three items, what led you to believe that others knew you were lesbian/bisexual?

_____

_____

_____

_____

188. I was open about my sexual orientation to other lesbians/bisexual women in the military.

Yes _____ No _____

If you identified as heterosexual for **any** part of the time you were on active duty please answer the following items, 189 to 192. If you identified **only** as lesbian/bisexual, skip to item 193.

189. I would have been uncomfortable sharing living quarters with someone I knew to be lesbian/bisexual.
  ____ 1. Strongly Disagree
  ____ 2. Disagree
  ____ 3. Uncertain
  ____ 4. Agree
  ____ 5. Strongly Agree

190. I would have been uncomfortable sharing a tent with someone I knew to be lesbian/bisexual.
  ____ 1. Strongly Disagree
  ____ 2. Disagree
  ____ 3. Uncertain
  ____ 4. Agree
  ____ 5. Strongly Agree

191. I knew military women who were lesbian/bisexual.
  Yes ____ No ____

192. I know women now who are lesbian/bisexual.
  Yes ____ No ____

193. Which of the following services/programs have you used?
  ____ 1. VA hospital
  ____ 2. VA housing loan
  ____ 3. VA educational benefits

_____ 4. College/university veterans offices

_____ 5. None

_____ 6. Other (describe) _____

194. Are there any particular problems that you can identity associated with using any of the above veterans services/programs? If yes, please describe. If no, skip to item 195.

_____

_____

_____

_____

195. Are there any particular problems that you can identify associated with being a woman veteran? If yes, please describe. If no, skip to item 196.

_____

_____

_____

_____

196. Which of the following best describes the way you heard about this study?

_____ 1. Veteran contact

(e.g., veteran/military organization, veteran/military publication, veteran/military gathering, veteran office, etc.)

_____ 2. Non-veteran contact

(e.g., non-veteran/military organization, non-veteran/military publication, bookstore, flyers, friends [veteran or not])

197. Are you familiar with the Women in Military Service for America Project?

Yes _____ No _____

198. Is there anything that I have not asked about that you would like to tell me about concerning your experience as a woman in the military?

_____

_____

_____

_____

_____

_____

_____

_____

_____

_____

NOTES

Notes to Chapter 1

1. For a more in-depth account of the entry of women into the military during World War II, see Melissa S. Herbert, "Amazons or Butterflies: The Recruitment of Women into the Military During World War II," pages 50–68 in *MINERVA: Quarterly Report on Women and the Military* 9(2) (Summer 1991).

2. Although members of the military are referred to as airmen (*sic*), sailors, Marines, and so on, dependent on their branch, for ease of discussion I use the term "soldiers," since the Army is the largest branch and in common parlance many refer to all members of the military as soldiers, regardless of branch.

3. There continues to be disagreement as to how the terms "sex" and "gender" should be used. Since the 1970s many have used "sex" to describe the physiological state of being female or male and "gender" to describe the sociocultural concepts of the feminine and the masculine (e.g., "She is feminine). The advent of West and Zimmerman's theoretical conceptualization of gender as a *process* adds to the confusion. Some may question the appropriateness of using "gender" as a sociocultural state of being *and* as a process. For ease of discussion I will use the term "gender" as both, though the broader theoretical positioning of my research is in gender as interactional, rather than as the "possession" of a set of attributes identified as feminine and/or masculine.

4. The term "ethnomethodology" is attributed to Harold Garfinkel. See Wallace and Wolf, *Contemporary Sociological The-*

ory, pp. 295–300, and Garfinkel's *Studies in Ethnomethodology* (Englewood Cliffs, N.J.: Prentice-Hall, 1967).

5. Suzanne Pharr's book, *Homophobia: A Weapon of Sexism* (Inverness, Calif.: Chardon Press, 1988) articulates this connection and was critical to my introduction to that link.

Notes to Chapter 2

1. While the ideal solution would be to eliminate the gendered nature of the occupational role, this research focuses on the very real problems encountered in a world where that is not the case. Thus, rather than speculate about how women might revolutionalize/feminize the military (Ruddick 1983), I have chosen to focus on their lives given the current constraints under which they operate.

2. Recent events such as the case of Lieutenant Kelly Flinn may be perceived as a challenge to this assertion. Nonetheless, in comparison to the other branches, I stand by my claim that the Air Force appears to be the most hospitable to women.

3. In her research on Army personnel, Laura Miller (personal communication, 1994) asked whether "being in the Army makes you less of a woman." Nine percent of women (N=964) said it does, 57 percent said it makes no difference, and 31 percent said it makes one more of a woman. When men (N=865) were asked whether "being in the Army makes a female soldier less of a woman," 21 percent said it does. Fifty-eight percent said it makes no difference, and 14 percent said it makes a female soldier more of a woman.

Notes to Chapter 3

1. Although commitment ceremonies, weddings, and similar celebrations have become popular among some lesbians and gay men, I refer here to the traditional wedding ritual of heterosexual women and men.

2. One example is the emphasis on male bonding within squad-level operations while simultaneously ridiculing men who are too

close to each other. Investigation of an explosion on the U.S.S. *Iowa* immediately focused on the alleged homosexual relationship between two friends who spent a great deal of time with each other rather than at strip clubs with "the guys." The Navy later retracted its accusations, albeit grudgingly.

Notes to Chapter 4

1. This figure might have been even higher if women had always been permitted to wear earrings. It was only in the 1980s that women were granted permission to wear earrings with certain dress uniforms.

2. In 1978, when I attended basic training, one woman brought a battery-operated, lighted makeup mirror on our field exercises.

3. The subsample used in this table is composed of those women who indicated that they had engaged in some type of closed-ended strategy. A given respondent was categorized as engaging in one of three types of strategies: feminine only, masculine only, or both feminine and masculine.

BIBLIOGRAPHY

Acker, Joan. 1992. "Gendered Institutions." *Contemporary Sociology* 21: 565–569.

———. 1990. "Hierarchies, Jobs, Bodies: A Theory of Gendered Organizations." *Gender & Society* 4: 139–158.

Amatea, Ellen S., and Margaret L. Fong-Beyette. 1987. "Through a Different Lens: Examining Professional Women's Interrole Coping By Focus and Mode." *Sex Roles* 17: 237–252.

Anderson, Marcia Kay. 1991. "Pioneer Women Athletic Trainers: Their Oppression and Resistance as Viewed from a Feminist Perspective." Ph.D. dissertation, Department of Physical Education. University of Iowa, Iowa City, Iowa.

Arkin, William, and Lynne R. Dobrofsky. 1978. "Military Socialization and Masculinity." *Journal of Social Issues* 34: 151–168.

Barkalow, Carol. 1990. *In the Men's House*. New York: Poseidon.

Benecke, Michelle M., and Kirstin S. Dodge. 1996. "Military Women: Casualties of the Armed Forces' War on Lesbians and Gay Men." Pp. 71–108 in *Gay Rights, Military Wrongs*, edited by Craig A. Rimmerman. New York: Garland.

Bevans, Margaret. 1960. *McCall's Book of Everyday Etiquette*. New York: Golden.

Blumenfeld, Warren J. 1992. "Squeezed into Gender Envelopes." Pp. 23–28 in *Homophobia: How We All Pay the Price*, edited by W. J. Blumenfeld. Boston: Beacon.

Burke, Carol. 1996. "Pernicious Cohesion." Pp. 205–219 in *It's Our Military Too! Women and the U.S. Military*, edited by Judith Hicks Stiehm. Philadelphia: Temple University Press.

Chodorow, Nancy. 1978. *The Reproduction of Mothering: Psychoanalysis and the Sociology of Gender*. Berkeley: University of California Press.

Chusmir, Leonard H., and Christine S. Koberg. 1990. "Dual Sex Role Identity and Its Relationship to Sex Role Conflict." *Journal of Psychology* 124: 545–555.

Cleeland, Nancy. 1993. "Military Gay Ban Harsher on Women Than on Men." *San Diego Union-Tribune*, 16 May, A1, A23.

Connell, Robert W. 1987. *Gender and Power*. Sydney: Allen and Unwin.

———. 1985. "Theorizing Gender." *Sociology* 19: 260–272.

Cordilia, Ann. 1983. *The Making of an Inmate: Prison as a Way of Life*. Cambridge, Mass.: Schenkman.

Curb, Rosemary, and Nancy Manahan. 1985. *Lesbian Nuns: Breaking Silence*. New York: Warner.

Dateline NBC. 1992. "Women in Combat." Produced by Christine Huneke, edited by Ina Smith.

Decker, Wayne. 1986. "Occupation and Impressions: Stereotypes of Males and Females in Three Professions." *Social Behavior and Personality* 14: 69–75.

DePauw, Linda Grant. 1988. "Gender as Stigma: Probing Some Sensitive Issues." *Minerva: Quarterly Report on Women and the Military* 6(1): 29–43.

Dienstfrey, Stephen J. 1989. "Who Serves in Combat: A Comparison of Men and Women Veterans with Service in War or Combat Zones." Paper presented at the meetings of the American Statistical Association, Washington, D.C.

Dunivin, Karen. 1994. "Military Culture: Change and Continuity." *Armed Forces and Society* 20: 531–547.

———. 1988. "There's Men, There's Women, and There's Me: The Role and Status of Military Women." *Minerva: Quarterly Report on Women and the Military* 6(2): 43–68.

Dunkle, John H., and Patricia L. Francis. 1990. "The Role of Facial Masculinity/femininity in the Attribution of Homosexuality." *Sex Roles* 23: 157–167.

Dyer, Kate. 1990. *Gays in Uniform: The Pentagon's Secret Reports.* Boston: Alyson.

Edwards, Paul N. 1990. "The Army and the Microworld: Computers and the Politics of Gender Identity." *Signs: Journal of Women in Culture and Society* 16: 102–127.

Enloe, Cynthia. 1993. *The Morning After: Sexual Politics at the End of the Cold War.* Berkeley: University of California Press.

———. 1989. *Bananas, Beaches, and Bases: Making Feminist Sense of International Politics.* Berkeley: University of California Press.

———. 1983. *Does Khaki Become You? The Militarization of Women's Lives.* Boston: South End Press.

Epstein, Cynthia Fuchs. 1990. "The Cultural Perspective and the Study of Work." Pp. 88–98 in *The Nature of Work: Sociological Perspectives,* edited by K. Erikson and S. P. Vallas. New Haven, Conn.: Yale University Press, American Sociological Association Presidential Series.

Epstein, Steven. 1994. "A Queer Encounter: Sociology and the Study of Sexuality." *Sociological Theory* 12: 188–202.

Faris, John H. 1975. "The Impact of Basic Combat Training." *Armed Forces and Society* 2: 115–127.

"Freedom of Press Seen on Trial Now." 1942. *New York Times,* 17 April, 8.

Gagnon, John H., and William Simon. 1973. *Sexual Conduct: The Sources of Human Sexuality.* Chicago: Aldine.

Gerber, Gwendolyn L. 1989. "The More Positive Evaluation of Men Than Women on the Gender-stereotyped Traits." *Psychological Reports* 65: 275–286.

Glidden, David. 1990. "Changing Weapons of Warfare Compel New Look at Gays, Women in the Army." *Los Angeles Times,* 17 June, M4, M8.

Goffman, Erving. 1977. "The Arrangement between the Sexes." *Theory and Society* 4: 301–331.

Gross, Jane. 1990. "Navy Is Urged to Root Out Lesbians Despite Abilities." *New York Times*, 2 September, 24.

Gutek, Barbara, Laurie Larwood, and Ann Stromberg. 1986. "Women at work." Pp. 217–234 in *International Review of Industrial and Organizational Psychology 1986*, edited by C. L. Cooper and I. Robertson. New York: Wiley.

Gutek, Barbara, and Bruce Morasch. 1982. "Sex Ratios, Sex-role Spillover and Sexual Harassment of Women at Work." *Journal of Social Issues* 38: 55–74.

Hall, Marny. 1986. "The Lesbian Corporate Experience." *Journal of Homosexuality* 12(3/4): 59–75.

Harris, Richard N. 1979. "Professionalization." Pp. 223–256 in *Socialization and the Life Cycle*, edited by P. I. Rose. New York: St. Martin's.

Harry, Joseph. 1984. "Homosexual Men and Women Who Served Their Country." *Journal of Homosexuality* 10: 117–125.

Holm, Jeanne. 1982. *Women in the Military: An Unfinished Revolution*. Novato, Calif.: Presidio.

Honey, Maureen. 1984. *Creating Rosie the Riveter: Class, Gender, and Propoganda during World War II*. Amherst: University of Massachusetts Press.

Hosek, James R., and Christine E. Peterson. 1990. *Serving Her Country: An Analysis of Women's Enlistment*. Prepared for the Office of the Assistant Secretary of Defense/Force Management and Personnel. Santa Monica, Calif.: RAND Corporation.

Humphrey, Mary Ann. 1990. *My Country, My Right to Serve*. New York: HarperCollins.

Jackson, Linda. 1983. "The Influence of Sex, Physical Attractiveness, Sex Role, and Occupational Sex-Linkage on Perceptions of Occupational Suitability." *Journal of Applied Social Psychology* 13: 31–44.

Kite, Mary E., and Kay Deaux. 1987. "Gender Belief Systems: Homosexuality and the Implicit Inversion Theory." *Psychology of Women Quarterly* 11: 83–96.

Lengermann, Patricia Madoo, and Ruth A. Wallace. 1985. *Gender in America: Social Control and Social Change*. Englewood Cliffs, N.J.: Prentice-Hall.

Lenskyj, Helen. 1986. *Out of Bounds: Women, Sport and Sexuality*. Toronto: Women's Press.

Lifton, Robert Jay. 1973. *Home from the War*. New York: Simon and Schuster.

Long, Bonita C., 1989. "Sex-role Orientation, Coping, Strategies, and Self-efficacy of Women in Traditional and Non-traditional Occupations." *Psychology of Women Quarterly* 13: 307–324.

Lowe, Maria R. 1993. "Beauty, Strength, and Grace: A Critical Analysis of Female Bodybuilding." Paper presented at the annual meetings of the American Sociological Association, Miami, Florida.

MacDonald, Sharon. 1987. "Drawing the Lines—Gender, Peace and War: An Introduction." Pp. 1–26 in *Images of Women in War and Peace: Cross-Cultural and Historical Perspectives*, edited by S. MacDonald, P. Holden, and S. Ardener. Madison: University of Wisconsin Press.

MacKinnon, Catharine A. 1982. "Feminism, Marxism, Method, and the State: An Agenda for Theory." *Signs* 7: 515–544.

Marshall, Kathryn. 1987. *In the Combat Zone: An Oral History of American Women in Vietnam 1966–1975*. Boston: Little, Brown.

Minerva's Bulletin Board. Spring 1994. "Proportion of Women Growing Among New Recruits," pp. 1–2.

———. Fall/Winter 1994. "Second Woman to Qualify as F-14 Pilot Dies in Crash," pp. 3–4.

Mitchell, Brian. 1989. *Weak Link: The Feminization of the American Military*. Washington, D.C.: Regnery Gateway.

Moskos, Charles. 1993. Chairman's Notes. *IUS Newsletter*. Chicago: Inter-University Seminar on Armed Forces and Society.

Novaco, Raymond, Thomas M. Cook, and Irwin G. Sarason. 1983. "Military Recruit Training: An Arena for Stress-coping Skills."

Pp. 377–418 in *Stress Reduction and Prevention*, edited by D. Meichenbaum and M. Jaremko. New York: Plenum.

Pellegrini, Ann. 1992. "S(h)ifting the Terms of Hetero/Sexism: Gender, Power, and Homophobias." Pp. 39–56 in *Homophobia: How We All Pay the Price*, edited by W. J. Blumenfeld. Boston: Beacon.

Perez, Julia. 1987. "Women Veterans Speak Out at the First Women in the Military Conference." *Minerva: Quarterly Report on Women and the Military* 5(3): 44–59.

Pharr, Suzanne. 1988. *Homophobia: A Weapon of Sexism*. Inverness, Calif.: Chardon.

Plummer, Kenneth. 1982. "Symbolic Interactionism and Sexual Conduct: An Emergent Perspective." Pp. 223–241 in *Human Sexual Relations: Towards a Redefinition of Sexual Politics*, edited by M. Brake. New York: Pantheon.

Radine, Lawrence B. 1977. *The Taming of the Troops: Social Control in the United States Army*. Westport, Conn.: Greenwood.

Rosenwasser, Shirley Miller, and Norma G. Dean. 1989. "Gender Role and Political Office: Effects of Perceived Masculinity/femininity of Candidate and Political Office." *Psychology of Women Quarterly* 13: 77–85.

Ruddick, Sara. 1983. "Pacifying the Forces: Drafting Women in the Interests of Peace." *Signs: Journal of Women and Culture in Society* 8: 471–489.

Schneider, Beth E. 1988. "Invisible and Independent: Lesbians' Experiences in the Workplace." Pp. 273–286 in *Women Working: Theories and Facts in Perspective*, 2d ed., edited by A. H. Stromberg and S. Harkess. Mountain View, Calif.: Mayfield.

Schneider, Dorothy, and Carl J. Schneider. 1988. *Sound Off: American Military Women Speak Out*. New York: Dutton.

Schur, Edwin M. 1984. *Labeling Women Deviant: Gender, Stigma, and Social Control*. Philadelphia: Temple University Press.

Segal, Mady Wechsler. 1978. "Women in the Military: Research and Policy Issues." *Youth and Society* 10: 101–126.

"Sexual Harassment: Where Does It End?" 1992. *Navy Times*, July 27, p. 22. Letter signed by Frank G. Williams.

Shatan, Chaim F. 1977. "Bogus Manhood, Bogus Honor: Surrender and Transfiguration in the United States Marine Corps." *Psychoanalytic Review* 64: 585–610.

Sheppard, Deborah L. 1989. "Organizations, Power and Sexuality: the Image and Self-Image of Women Managers." Pp. 139–157 in *The Sexuality of Organization*, edited by J. Hearn, D. L. Sheppard, P. Tancred-Sheriff, and G. Burrell. London: Sage.

Shilts, Randy. 1993. *Conduct Unbecoming: Gays and Lesbians in the U.S. Military*. New York: St. Martin's.

Siann, Gerda. 1994. *Gender, Sex, and Sexuality: Contemporary Psychological Perspectives*. Bristol, Pa.: Taylor and Francis.

Steinberg, Ronnie. 1992. "Gender on the Agenda: Male Advantage in Organizations." *Contemporary Sociology* 21: 576–581.

Stiehm, Judith Hicks. 1989. *Arms and the Enlisted Woman*. Philadelphia: Temple University Press.

Stivers, Camilla. 1993. *Gender Images in Public Administration: Legitimacy and the Administrative State*. Newbury Park, Calif.: Sage.

Swerdlow, Marian. 1989. "Men's Accommodations to Women Entering a Nontraditional Occupation: A Case of Rapid Transit Operatives." *Gender and Society* 3: 373–387.

Tetreault, Mary Ann. 1988. "Gender Belief Systems and the Integration of Women in the U.S. Military." *Minerva: Quarterly Report on Women and the Military* 6(1): 44–71.

Treadwell, Mattie. 1953. *The Women's Army Corps*. United States Army in World War II: Special Studies. Washington, D.C.: Office of the Chief of Military History, Department of the Army.

Vazquez, Carmen. 1992. "Appearances." Pp. 157–166 in *Homophobia: How We All Pay the Price*, edited W. J. Blumenfeld. Boston: Beacon.

Veterans Administration. 1985. *Survey of Female Veterans: A Study of the Needs, Attitudes, and Experiences of Women Veterans.*

Office of Information Management and Statistics, IM&S M 70-85-7.

Wallace, Ruth A., and Alison Wolf. 1991. *Contemporary Sociological Theory: Continuing the Classical Tradition.* Englewood Cliffs, N.J.: Prentice-Hall.

Warner, Rebecca. 1985. "The Impact of Military Service on the Early Career: An Extension of the Bridging Environment Hypothesis to Women." Ph.D. dissertation, Department of Sociology, Washington State University, Pullman.

Weeks, Jeffrey. 1986. *Sexuality.* New York: Routledge.

Weitz, Rose. 1989. "What Price Independence? Social Reactions to Lesbians, Spinsters, Widows, and Nuns." Pp. 446–456 in *Women: A Feminist Perspective,* 4th ed., edited by J. Freeman. Mountain View, Calif.: Mayfield.

West, Candace, and Sarah Fenstermaker. 1993. "Power, Inequality and the Accomplishment of Gender: An Ethnomethodological View." Pp. 151–174 in *Theory on Gender/Feminism on Theory,* edited by P. England. Hawthorne, N.Y.: Aldine de Gruyter.

West, Candace, and Don H. Zimmerman. 1987. "Doing Gender." *Gender and Society* 1: 125–151.

Wharton, Amy S., and James N. Baron. 1987. "So Happy Together? The Impact of Gender Segregation on Men at Work." *American Sociological Review* 52: 574–587.

Wheelwright, Julie. 1989. *Amazons and Military Maids: Women Who Dressed as Men in Pursuit of Life, Liberty and Happiness.* London: Pandora.

Williams, Christine L. 1989. *Gender Differences at Work: Women and Men in Nontraditional Occupations.* Berkeley: University of California Press.

Wilson, George C. 1989. *Mud Soldiers.* New York: Scribners.

Woods, James D. 1993. *The Corporate Closet: The Professional Lives of Gay Men in America.* New York: Free Press.

Yarmolinksy, Adam 1971. *The Military Establishment*. New York: Harper and Row.

Yoder, Janice D., and Jerome Adams. 1984. "Women Entering Nontraditional Roles: When Work Demands and Sex-Roles Conflict: The Case of West Point." *International Journal of Women's Studies* 7: 260–272.

INDEX

ABOUT THE AUTHOR

Melissa S. Herbert received her Ph.D. from the University of Arizona in 1995. She served in the enlisted ranks of the United States Army and later attended Officer Candidate School at Fort Benning, Georgia.

Dr. Herbert is Assistant Professor of Sociology at Hamline University in Saint Paul, Minnesota where she teaches courses on gender, sexuality, and social psychology, as well as a first year seminar on HIV/AIDS. Her other research interests include issues of gender and sexuality in friendship and in sport.